GOODBYE HOOP SKIRTS - HELLO WORLD!

The Travels, Triumphs and Tumbles
Of A Runaway Southern Belle

MARY MOORE MASON

TSL Publications

First published in Great Britain in 2021
By TSL Publications, Rickmansworth

Copyright © 2021 Mary Moore Mason

ISBN / 978-1-914245-17-6

Cover design by Dave Houghton
Front cover image copyright Masson-Shutterstockcom
Back cover image: Geoff Moore/The Travel Trunk

"I shall be telling this with a sigh
Somewhere ages and ages hence:
Two roads diverged in a wood and I–
I took the one less traveled by,
And this has made all the difference."
... *The Road Not Taken,* Robert Frost.

Dedicated to Mark, Wendy, Little Rose and Miz Rose and all the other family and friends who have been my inspiration and guardian angels over many a decade.

Special thanks to David Houghton for the cover design, sub-editors Stewart Wild and Neil Murray and my publisher Anne Samson of TSL Publications.

In 1950's Southern Belle mode

Introduction

When I was growing up in the racially-segregated American South, a young Southern lady could reach the top of the pole by being a cheerleader, beauty queen or the belle of an Old South ball. She might idolize *Gone with the Wind's* spirited Scarlett O'Hara with her 21-inch waist and crinoline-covered hoop skirts only to become a docile Melanie Wilkes, if briefly, when she married her high school or college sweetheart. And if she ever spent time with a person of color it was probably the family maid.

Although I, too, was directed toward Southern belledom, my path headed off in a different direction. Perhaps it was genetically preordained: my mother, a rebel against domesticity, was descended from a courageous survivor of American Indian captivity, and my father worked his way through college during the Great Depression by running a jazz band. Be that as it may, after maneuvering myself into the all-male newsroom of a Virginia newspaper, which was dedicated to preserving racial segregation, I spent many an evening attending racially-mixed parties organized by my Jewish boyfriend from "up North".

Inspired by a mind-expanding university trip throughout Europe, I then bought a one-way ticket to Paris to reignite a summer romance with a handsome young Frenchman – and decamped with his Sicilian-American friend to become a travel writer in Athens. Next stop: 1960's "Swinging London" where I later married a British photographer known for his photos of the Beatles and the great American jazz musicians.

It was a great time and a great place to establish new careers in both journalism and international tourism promotion. Pan American World Airways, which I joined as the Public

The author as a globe-trotting travel writer

Relations (Press) representative, was on the cusp of revolutionizing transatlantic tourism by launching the world's first Boeing 747 "Jumbo Jet". Then came the UK media relations for four other pioneering airlines; the US Travel Service; the Aga Khan's collection of majestic European hotels; and the state of Texas just as *Dallas* and the fractious Ewing family, their friends and foes burst onto TV screens around the world.

Topping it all off was the opportunity to become the launching editor of *Holiday USA & Canada*, the UK's first travel magazine focusing on North America, and its successor, *Essentially America*, which I have now edited for more than 25 years.

However, my story doesn't begin or end there but on a Shenandoah Valley cattle farm founded by my Scots-Irish ancestors in 1735 ... my place of refuge in turbulent times, with side trips to my childhood homes in Roanoke, Virginia, the "Star City of the South", the small West Virginia river town where my grandparents resided, and to the Notting Hill, London, townhouse where I have lived for more than three decades.

Are these tales worth sharing or just my self-absorbed ramble down Memory Lane?

Please read on and decide for yourself.

Contents

Carry Me Back To Ole Virginny

This was to be a special day – my first day living in tranquil rural Virginia after 19 years in action-packed London – but what followed was a bit of a surprise. As I drove up the country lane to the base of the hill crowned by Walkerlands, our ancestral family home, Mark, age 7, called out from the back seat: "Look mum! Why are those big, black birds circling granny's house?" "Don't know," I muttered, as we ascended the gravel drive, "but I don't think it's good news." And there, in the side pasture at the brow of the hill, were four very dead cows, flat on their backs, their hooves raised to heaven.

Unlocking the back door of the frame farmhouse and entering my mother's bedroom, I rather laconically said: "Great to see you, mother. Have you noticed the dead cows in the side pasture?"

Arising from her bed in an elegant, floral, silk dressing gown, a book in one hand, a gin and tonic in the other, she hugged us both and replied: "Yes, darling. Isn't the smell awful? I just have to keep all the doors closed and spray the room with Chanel No 5."

"Why hasn't Sid done something about it?" I queried, referring to the local farmer my mother had gone into the cattle business with after my father died. "Oh, my dear, he can't," she replied. "He and Anne are on a Caribbean cruise and that farmhand he used hasn't been the same since he got Agent Oranged in Vietnam, so Sid let him go."

"Well then, why didn't you do something about it?" I grumbled. "Because," she replied, indignantly, "that's man's work and I, my dear, am a Southern lady."

Welcome home to Virginia, the land of the Southern belle, I thought as I put down my suitcase and phoned Pete, the former Walkerlands farmhand.

"I'm not surprised them there cows died," said Pete. "That Sid, he didn't know shit about raising cattle, so I'm glad I ain't working with him no more." Assured that Sid was at least temporarily out of the picture, and offered a tempting financial reward, Pete came to the rescue, chatting with me while he dug a trench with a backhoe, dumped the cattle in and covered them with quicklime.

"I told that Sid he should build a fence around them wild cherry trees," said Pete. "When the cows eat the leaves they blow up and die."

As he went off to string barbed-wire fencing around the offending trees, I considered the possibility that my years as a London-based travel writer, magazine editor and airline industry publicist might not have equipped me for the realities of farm life.

So I phoned my Texas-born neighbor Steve Heffelfinger who, as a cattle-raiser and "kissing kin" (as distant cousins are known in Virginia), might prove to be particularly helpful. His eyes shielded by a moth-eaten old Stetson and accompanied by two hound dogs he addressed as Fidel Castro and Che Guevara, Steve arrived in a rickety pick-up truck and summoned me to clamber in. And as we bounced through the pastures, surrounded by cattle, he said in his Texas drawl: "Wow, Cuzin Mary, you sure got a shit load of problems here. See that little heifer over there? She bin running with the bulls too young. That cow there has a cancer in her eye and that other one has a limpy leg. About the only thing good here is that big ole bull.

"How come your mother being city folks wants to have a herd of Black Angus cows?" he added, and I explained that although Dad (who loved puns) always said he would never "play the stock market" when they retired to Walkerlands,

Walkerlands, home to six generations of my family

Mary Moore and Mark enjoying rural life

My mother, also named Mary Moore, the mistress of Walkerlands

mother decided after his death she'd rather be known as a lady rancher than a retired schoolteacher. And then she loved sitting on the back veranda at twilight, sipping her gin and tonic and watching "my cattle parade march by".

"Well, be that as it may, I would sell the lot and get out of the cattle business," advised Steve. So, a couple of weeks later a meeting was arranged with a truculent Sid, who agreed to move his half of the herd elsewhere, whereas our half was auctioned off, making a miniscule profit.

So why, you might ask, was I there anyway? Therein hangs a much longer tale, but here's the short version: after moving to London in the "Swinging Sixties", marrying a British photographer, becoming a stepmother and then mother, leading a fun-filled but sometimes challenging personal and professional life and then getting divorced, I decided my lifestyle was a bit like tap dancing through the mine fields. It would be therapeutic for me and Mark to experience the tranquility of rural life.

Of course I would miss my old life as the founding editor of Britain's first North American-focused travel magazine, *Holiday USA & Canada*, the London-based PR for the USA tourism office and the media midwife for Pan Am's Boeing 747, the world's first "Jumbo Jet", and the whole follow-on flock of brand-new transatlantic airlines known as "the darlings of deregulation". But surely it was time for a whole new life and career back in my native USA.

Jump Mountain overshadowing Walkerlands is the site of a local Native American legend

Laurel and Hardy's Contribution
To the Shenandoah Valley

The lovely lyrics of the old folk song *Oh Shenandoah, I long to see you and hear your rolling river* may warm the romantic hearts of many residents of this 200-mile-long valley in western Virginia ... with a small overlap into West Virginia ... but it's the wacky rendition of *The Trail of the Lonesome Pine* in the 1937 Laurel and Hardy film *Way Out West* that most people associate with the region. As they twang away to the lyrics "In the Blue Ridge Mountains of Virginia", Ollie bangs Stan on the head with a mallet and he erupts into a falsetto before keeling over. In any case, the valley, whose name, shared with its river, allegedly comes from a Native American word meaning "beautiful daughter of the stars", is best known for its surrounding Blue Ridge and Appalachian mountains, picturesque college towns, Civil War battlefield sites, awesome caves, cattle farms and apple orchards. Many of those farms, such as Walkerlands, were settled in the 1730s by Scots-Irish and German immigrants who traveled down its Great Wagon Road, later Route 11, now paralleled by hyper-busy Interstate 81. A few of them, including some of my family as you will later learn, had traumatic encounters with the Native Americans.

As for my mother, she had her own reason for remaining on this beautiful but isolated farm, 18 miles of winding mountain road from Lexington, the closest town of any size. It was primarily emotional; although she had grown up in my grandfather's small town in West Virginia, she had spent every summer of her girlhood back here at Walkerlands, her mother's family home on farmland settled in 1735 by her Scots-Irish immigrant ancestors. Also, my late father had loved the place and spent his final years bringing it back to life.

A Nibble of the "Big Apple"

My real home was not Walkerlands but Roanoke, about an hour-and-a-half's drive south from Lexington and the region's largest city. Once known as Big Lick, reputedly because of the salt licks for cattle in the area, Roanoke seemed to have an inferiority complex. That's probably because it had none of the colonial or Civil War cachet of many other Virginia towns and cities. So, in my childhood, the city fathers decided to put it on the map by installing a huge neon star on the top of its tallest mountain so it could become known as "The Star City of the South" as well as "The Magic City".

Our rather charming white frame house with green shutters and dormer windows – the first my parents ever owned – was nestled in a little valley at the base of a steep hill. It was backed by a deep woodland where I frequently played cowboys and Indians with the neighboring children. The house was always full of music – my father, an insurance executive, was a talented pianist who had worked his way through college running a dance band so it was not unusual to get a bit of early-morning ragtime before he departed for work.

Our family home in Roanoke, Virginia

Meanwhile my mother, who had temporarily put her teaching career on hold, conjured up delicious meals and dreamed of someday becoming a published short-story writer. My elementary school was within walking distance; I loved my pretty first grade teacher Miss Lavender; and all was right with the world.

Then everything changed. Dad was summoned to New York City for basic training as a World War II naval officer and mother and I joined him for the final days before he was shipped off to places unknown. Comfortably housed in an apartment overlooking Central Park, we spent time each day stretched out on the living room floor while dad, with the aid of a pen and ruler, divided maps of the world into numbered squares, 1a, 1b, etc. In his letters home, he explained, he would reveal in a code exactly which square he was in. It was totally forbidden, he added, for us to let anyone else know as the enemy might be watching and waiting for this type of information.

Dad regularly serenaded us on the piano

While dad was off training, mother and I went to Central Park where I became friendly with the first Asian person I had ever met, a beautiful little Chinese girl with whom I played hide and seek among the trees and beside the lake. Her mother explained to mine that she had been born in New York, went to a special theater school and was, in fact, dancing that very evening with the local ballet. My parents bought tickets ... and there she was in the center of the stage portraying a magical bluebird weaving in and out between the legs of the elegant ballerinas.

Before our time in "The Big Apple" ended, we visited Radio City Music Hall with its awesome high-kicking Rockettes, the Museum of Modern Art, where I was fascinated by the melting clocks in Salvador Dali's *Persistence of Memory,* and Coney Island, where dad took me on a short but thrilling roller-coaster ride. Someday, I vowed, I am going to live in a city like this.

The two Mary Moores

Dad goes off to World War II

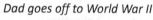

Central Park's Strawberry Fields tribute to John Lennon
(Photo: Willy Wong/NYC & Co)

𝔒he Charisma of Central ℙark

America's most-famous, most-visited urban park, encompassing 843 acres, about 340 acres larger than the country of Monaco – was not only a magnet for me then but in recent years for my young granddaughter, Rose, who loved tire-swinging and zipping down a slide in the Diana Ross playground, named after the famous Supremes diva who lives nearby; my German-born step-grandson Dominik, who spent at least an hour feeding popcorn to the baby turtles swarming out of the park lake; and his older sister Lara, who was photographed sitting in the midst of the John Lennon tributary *Imagine* artwork. It was installed in the park area renamed *Strawberry Fields* by Lennon's widow, Yoko Ono, after he was gunned down by a disgruntled fan on December 8, 1980, in front of their nearby Dakota apartment. It is close to the one in which my family and I stayed all those decades ago.

Heritage and Harassment in West Virginia

When we returned to Roanoke, mother decided we could no longer live in our beloved new house on dad's reduced salary, so she put it on the rental market. The first potential resident was a nice young married man who, because of a health problem, was unable to go to war, but when our next-door neighbors discovered he was Jewish, they told my mother he would not be welcome in the neighborhood and certainly not as their next-door neighbor. Deeply distressed, mother felt obligated to tell the young man and he moved on and so did we ... to live with my grandparents in West Virginia.

Sandwiched between high West Virginia mountains and the Kanawha River, the small college town of Montgomery had been founded and named after my ancestors, whose antecedents, I suspect, would have been rather surprised to find their descendants in this off-the-beaten-path community of no great note. For, according to reasonably well-documented family accounts, they were Scandinavian Gomeriks who, in the ninth century, invaded Normandy, where they settled on a hill and thus became the Mons Gomeriks.

In 1066, one Roger de Montgomerie joined William the Conqueror in the invasion of England, being given as a reward land therein and the title Earl of Shrewsbury, Arundel and Chichester. His descendants prospered, spreading into Wales, Scotland and, eventually, Northern Ireland, from which our ancestor, Henry Montgomery, emigrated to America. Serving as a major in the Virginia militia, he was awarded land on both sides of the Kanawha River, where his son, James, founded Montgomery.

The Two Virginias - Separated Siblings

Best known to many today as the inspiration for the John Denver version of the ballad *Take Me Home, Country Roads*, the scenic but financially-challenged Mountain State has the distinction of being the only one born out of the American Civil War. Long disgruntled by what it considered the lack of attention from the Virginia state government based in far-away Richmond, it declared independence in 1863 and, because of its divided loyalties, found brothers fighting against brothers, fathers against sons in that bloodiest of all American conflicts. My Virginia born-and-bred grandmother felt she was going very downmarket when she agreed to marry my West Virginia grandfather and then only after he agreed she could spend part of each year back in Virginia.

The patriarch of the West Virginia Montgomery clan was Seth, the much-older brother and guardian of my grandfather, whose parents had both died when he was a child. Seth, who from his photograph looked rather like a severe Mark Twain, ruled the roost from one of the grander, white-columned houses in town which he shared with his heiress daughter Julia, my grandfather, Frederick Hale Montgomery, Fred's Virginia-born wife Fannie Moore (nee Walker) and, in her childhood, my mother, like me, named Mary Moore.

Julia, sent away to be educated in a posh finishing school, was thought by her father to be too grand to marry anyone locally so upon her return she waited for many years until he died to marry her long-term suitor, Brown Carpenter, the successful owner of the local hardware store. When he died years later she, rather like Miss Havisham in *Great Expectations,* lived alone with her memories, the furniture swathed in dust sheets, the chandeliers draped with spider webs.

Off to school in a new state

*My grandfather Montgomery
as a young man*

While she was still young, my grandparents and mother moved to a quaint wooden cottage that was separated from Uncle Seth's home by a back garden, its wide front porch lined with rocking chairs from which we could overlook the comings and goings of two sets of cousins living in twin brick homes across the street. Their homes, in turn, backed onto the river which, said my mother, had in her youth been visited by show boats producing harrowing melodramas of feckless parents and virginal daughters threatened by dastardly villains.

It was in Montgomery that my mother, then in her first year as a local schoolteacher, met my dad, who was attending the local West Virginia University Institute of Technology on a music scholarship while, as a pianist, running the college dance band named Bob Mason and his Collegians. After transferring to and graduating from the more prestigious North Carolina State University in the height of the Great Depression, he was hired as a claims manager by Boston-based Liberty Mutual Insurance Company, married my mother and they moved to Louisville, Kentucky, where I was born. Later homes included Nashville, Tennessee; Jacksonville, Florida; and finally, Roanoke, Virginia.

As I got to know my stately, rather-saintly Montgomery grandfather, I discovered that he had been a rather naughty young boy. Sent to military school at a young age, he regularly ran away to ride the rails, much to the ire of both the school and his family. Now retired from the family insurance business, which he disliked, he focused on helping run a little Presbyterian chapel in a nearby mining town and on exercising his love of trains.

On most days, dressed in a long black coat, crowned by a jaunty Homburg and mysteriously followed by the family cat, he would escort me to the town railroad station. There, he would produce a large gold pocket watch and time the trains. Upon their arrival, there would be consultations with the African-American conductors who all seemed to have Old Testament names – Moses, Joshua, Aaron. "Yas sir, Mr Fred and Little Missy," one of them might say, "da train got slowed down in de tunnel. Sweet Jesus knows why."

Meanwhile, I regularly received thrilling and exotic gifts from my naval officer father: a grass skirt from Hawaii, a small wooden fishing boat from the Philippines, a doll from somewhere in south-east Asia, silver coins for me and jewelry for mother from India, while she, using the coded maps, searched diligently for dad's whereabouts.

Other aspects of Montgomery life were not as pleasant. For some reason, my elementary school mates, Nat and Hugh Kennedy, apparently egged on by two of my young cousins, decided that I was an interloper in their territory and would regularly rough me up on my way home from school. Fed up one wintry day, I stuffed rocks in my snowballs, aimed carefully at Nat, and hit him in the nose. Blood flowed freely and, both crying, we fled to our respective homes.

Once there, I was hesitant to explain to my grandfather, a Presbyterian elder and an avowed pacifist, what I had done but when he finally discovered the truth, he patted me on the head, said everyone needed to learn when to stand up for themselves, and took me to the popular town hang-out, Eddie Kelly's Drug Store, for a chocolate-nut sundae. I had no trouble thereafter coming home safely from school.

—World-News Staff Photo

GREETINGS—Mary Moore Mason poses prettily with a giant-size heart, a reminder that tomorrow is Valentine's Day. It is also "Heart Sunday" and donations to the Heart Fund campaign will be collected between 2 and 4 p.m. Mary Moore is the daughter of Mr. and Mrs. R. E. Mason, 2735 Stephenson Ave., SW.

Valentine's Day fame in
The Roanoke Times

Theatrical Misadventures

When World War II ended, we returned to Roanoke where, perhaps inspired by my brief time in Manhattan or dad's tales of his travels, I kept longing to be somewhere else. Sometimes I would slip away from the back of the house, follow a path through the woodlands to the highway and, seated on a small hill, enthusiastically wave at the passing cars. If someone waved back I knew they would take the memory of me – the little girl on the hill – to wherever they were going and I, in effect, would be there too … perhaps back in New York, in China or some other place all the way across America or on the other side of the world.

I slept in an upstairs room overlooking the one-storey car port attached to the house and awoke one night to a terrible crashing noise. Leaping from bed and peering out the window, I discovered the car port now lay on its side astride the family car. As my bewildered parents and I gathered in the front yard we saw a distraught-looking man racing down the hill and shouting "Has anyone seen my truck?" With amazing calm, my father replied: "It appears to be having a romance with part of my house."

When dad discovered the driver had no insurance but was a carpenter, he suggested he rebuild the car port. This he did over the next few weeks, regularly reinforced by periods on other work projects and trays of sandwiches and cold drinks served by my mother.

At night, dad studied law and, after passing the Virginia Bar exam, was asked to set up a law practice with a friend. However, much to my mother's dismay, he declined the offer out of loyalty to the insurance company that had given him that coveted job during the Great Depression. Although mother was keen to return to her life as a schoolteacher, dad, she said, insisted she should be a stay-at-home mum, which she appeared to regard as a form of domestic servitude. One night dad came bustling home from the office and shouted: "What's for supper?" as he opened and then slammed the oven door, causing the cake therein to fall. Mother removed it from the oven, took careful aim, threw it across the kitchen and it went splat on dad's back.

However, that aside, it was a happy life, both at home and at school. My first journalistic experience was a column of local events for *The Chatterbox* newspaper, which several of us created in elementary school – one of my friend's dads photocopied it in his office and we sold it for a nickel a copy. Also a keen artist, in middle school I began reproducing drawings from the semi-nude girlie magazines and selling them to the boys in my class. When my horrified teacher discovered my fledgling business, she reported it to the principal, who summoned my mother to the school. As I sat fearfully outside her office door, amazingly there were sounds of great merriment coming from within and I was simply told to go and sin no more.

In high school, I disgraced myself by throwing spit balls made of moistened rolled-up paper at a friend across the room while our formidable teacher, Miss Virginia Page, had her back to the class as she chalked up notes on the blackboard. As punishment, I was kept after school and forced to write long essays about *Hamlet* and *Macbeth*. At the end of my week-long ordeal, Miss Page said that, although I was a very difficult girl, I seemed to have some writing talent. Thus, I was put down for a creative writing course jointly taught – frequently incompatibly – by a middle-aged prima dona, whose taste vered toward the frothy and romantic, and a feisty Northern transplant who favored the grittier, more-realistic form of contemporary literature.

Along the way, I acted in school plays, usually in comedy roles, although one Valentine's Day, enhanced by a splendid blonde wig and with padding in my bra, I portrayed Marilyn Monroe while rather seductively (if off-key) singing *Diamonds Are A Girl's Best Friend*. My photo, clutching a box of heart-shaped candy and unfortunately sans wig, then appeared in the local newspapers.

But perhaps my most memorable theatrical appearances were in the local Presbyterian church's nativity plays. Held outdoors over Christmas week and featuring not only a large cast of costumed children but also live animals, the productions were a real crowd-puller, so it was a great honor to be cast one year as the Angel Gabriel.

Hoisted on to the church roof, my head encircled by a tinsel halo and looking quite obese in layers of warm clothing topped by a white robe, I was strapped to a cross which was attached to the church roof. This, I was told, would provide both safety and the illusion that my arms and wings were spread out in blessing to the Holy Family far below. Alas, as the spotlight focused on me and *Hark, the Herald Angels Sing* boomed out on the church speakers, it began to snow and the wind to blow. The heavy cross became detached and I found myself lurching along the roof like the Hunchback of Notre Dame. The lights went off, the music stopped and I was rescued by the always-grumpy Director of Christian Education (it was said her bad temper was induced by the fact she had an unrequited passion for the Youth Minister).

But more humiliation was on its way a couple of years later when I was cast as the Virgin Mary. Seated in a stable made of bales of hay I was required to gaze in adoration at a light bulb hidden in the manger which, with its upward glow, represented the Baby Jesus. Seated across from me, Joseph was portrayed by a freckle-faced, red-haired – and foul-mouthed – little boy named Jimmy Bullington. Suddenly the donkey nibbling the surrounding hay apparently nibbled him on the elbow. Leaping to his feet and overturning the manger during which "Baby Jesus" exploded, he tore off his "Yasser Arafat" headdress, threw it on the ground and shouted out an obscenity describing what he thought God should do to a monkey. Then, as he marched off down the street, rapidly followed by the alarmed donkey and several sheep, the nativity play reached its unexpected but dramatic finale.

There were, of course, high school romances – with the handsome but dumb football hero whose mother was a truck driver; the bore who insisted on telling me the most naff jokes as we fox-trotted at the school prom; and the bright, amusing but bossy boy who never forgave me for refusing to "go steady" by dating him alone and wearing his high school fraternity pin.

It was also a period of an evolving social consciousness. One night a bunch of us, crammed into a convertible, arrived at the local hamburger joint and, after taking our order, the gum-chewing roller-skating waitress stopped briefly by a neighboring car containing an African-American man, his wife and two small children. "We don't serve niggers here," she said. "But lady," the father replied in a weary voice, "we've been driving a long way, my children are hungry and nobody will serve us."

"That's not my problem," she snapped, skating away and the black family left. "Why didn't I do something? Why didn't I jump out, stop them, order for them," I agonized to myself. But it was too late … and nobody else in the car had even seemed to notice.

Then there was the plight of Stella McLean, the proud, dignified, half-black, half-Cherokee lady who weekly came to our house to clean, iron and help with the cooking. Gradually, she confided in my mother what her life was like. Her husband was a usually unemployed drunkard who regularly roughed her up and took most of her earnings; her hopes all lay with her teenage daughter completing high school and getting a job. Then the girl got pregnant, left the baby with Stella and became a prostitute.

One day Stella didn't show up for work. Another day passed and she was absent again. Concerned, mother called around and found Stella had mentally broken down but nobody knew where she was. Years later when I had my first newspaper job covering, among other things, mental health, I tracked her down to Western State Lunatic Hospital in Staunton, Virginia. Visiting her, I asked if she remembered me and my mother. She nodded yes but her eyes said no, and I realized her whole painful past was now clouded in the mists of time.

*Our high school prom was held at the grand Hotel
Roanoke, now on the National Registry of Historic Places
(Photo: The Hotel Roanoke & Convention Center)*

*Historic Roanoke market
(Photo: Cameron Davidson/Visit VBR)*

Off to University in North Carolina

When it was time for college, I decided on the University of North Carolina, which, reputedly, had an outstanding journalism school. There was just one problem – it wouldn't take women until their junior year, so I headed instead to Charlotte, North Carolina's Queens College, my mother's alma mater. Set in a lovely residential area of the city, it proved in many ways ideal – good teachers and small enough to allow the formation of lifelong friendships, among them with my room mate, Roxana Mebane. She took me sailing near her home on the Carolina coast, taught me how to water-ski, later became president of the student body and, after graduation, married a Presbyterian preacher and eventually herself became the pastor of an African-American church in Washington, DC.

Transferring to UNC in Chapel Hill, I took such courses as feature writing, libel and the law and photography while working on the *Daily Tar Heel* where, as features editor, I got first choice of interviews with visiting speakers such as poet Robert Frost and evangelist Billy Graham. Meanwhile, inspired by my bohemian room mate Nancy, I had a fling at college theatricals portraying a happy hooker in New Orleans whose only duet with another "hooker" was entitled *Selling Is All We Do*. (My parents, who had attended expecting something like *The Sound of Music* or *Brigadoon*, were not impressed.)

I particularly loved my literature and history courses but was so hopeless in economics that I had to take the course again in summer school, an idyllic time when I could lie by the local lake reading my way through the American and English classics.

29

North Carolina and Its Pioneering University

If Sir Walter Raleigh's "Lost Colony", established on the coast of North Carolina in 1587, had survived, it would have been lauded as the birthplace of English-speaking America. Instead, it mysteriously disappeared without a trace or sign of struggle three years later leaving Jamestown, Virginia, settled twenty years later, to claim the fame. Nevertheless, the state has numerous other delightful and historic towns and cities, not only along the coast and across its center but also along the legendary Blue Ridge Parkway, which wends its way along North Carolina's western mountain tops. And, most importantly to me, it is home to America's oldest public university, founded in 1795 and based in the small city of Chapel Hill. As I completed this book, I learned that the university has finally accepted the fact that many of its founders were vehement and often-violent segregationists by stripping their names off and renaming many of the campus buildings.

And then there were the boyfriends. My sorority sisters chose traditional beaus and were appropriately rewarded. One beauty, chosen as the "Sweetheart of Sigma Chi" fraternity, was serenaded by moonlight from the balcony of our sorority house by her boyfriend and all the fraternity brothers and then given a beautiful bunch of roses and a diamond engagement ring. Instead, I got strange presents from my beaus.

One was a baby chicken, which I kept in a shoe box under my bed and named Zelda – we were all reading Scott Fitzgerald at the time. As it grew, we discovered it was in fact a rooster that became unpopular when it crowed the whole house awake each dawn. I took it home to my parents who, after the neighbors complained about its vocal range, bequeathed it to our maid, Wookie, with the understanding she would take Zelda to her rural home and see it came to no harm. Later, she claimed hunters had shot Zelda out of a tree; I suspected she and her family had eaten Zelda for Sunday lunch.

Later, I inadvertently got my own back on Wookie when another beau, a medical student whom I had semi-rebuffed, presented me with a boxed gift upon my departure home for spring break, making me promise not to open it until I arrived in Roanoke. When I did, I was horrified to find it was a fetal baby floating in a bottle which my admirer had obviously stolen from one of the medical school labs. I quickly hid it at the back of my clothes closet and forgot about it until Wookie came roaring down the steps shouting at my mother, "Miz Mary Moore, Miz Mary Moore, come quickly. I found a little baby bopping around in a bottle in Little Miz Mary Moore's closet!"

After being reassured by me that the baby was not mine, my parents were remarkably calm. "We must give this child a Christian burial," said my father. So, one moonless night, armed with flash lights, the Bible and a spade, we crept into the woodlands at the back of the house and buried the baby. From time to time in years thereafter I fretted that someone might find it and we'd all be taken to jail. In any case, the medical student was thereafter no longer part of my social circle.

Wookie frequently told us stories of her church's inspiring pastor who not only preached powerful sermons but also had an impressive set of gold teeth. "I tell you, Miz Mary Moore," she would tell my mother, "the glory of God shines out of that man's mouth!" Then one day she arrived grinning from ear to ear and, pulling back her lips, indicated her own, new gold tooth. "But, Wookie," I protested, "it's at the back so nobody can see it!" "It don't matter," she replied, "I knows it's there and Sweet Jesus knows it's there ... and that's all that matters!"

Back to UNC, I generally found the fraternity boys a waste of time ... all they seemed interested in was partying, drinking, holding panty raids on the girls' dormitories and driving around town in open sports cars while flashing their bums (known as

Romantic, Rebellious South Carolina

Not only were the hot-headed South Carolinians credited with beginning the American Civil War on April 12, 1861, when they fired on Union-held Fort Sumter in Charleston's harbor but the Confederate flag was still flying in Columbia's State House grounds until July 10, 2015. Today, it is rightly no longer politically correct to romanticize the "Lost Cause" of the Confederacy but you can still fall in love, as I have, with the state's charming old cities, beguiling resort islands, scrumptious cuisine and lush, sub-tropical gardens. On one of my more recent visits I even attended a family wedding on a plantation owned by the late husband of my first cousin, Kay Maybank, noting that although the beautiful manor house was destroyed during the Civil War, the avenue of slave cabins remains. One day years before, said Kay, her parents-in-law were approached by the elderly daughter of a former slave who asked to move into one of the cabins. "I was born here and I wants to die here," she said. And the Maybanks made her comfortable as she settled in.

Touring charming old Charleston, South Carolina, in the traditional way

mooning) at unimpressed bystanders. Meanwhile, my two South Carolina aunts were doing their best to match me up with what they considered to be nice young men from good Southern families.

Aunt Katherine's romantic candidate for me, a rather good-looking but boring young man named Bob, invited me to be his date for the University of South Carolina Old South Ball. This always began, he explained, with a march down the main street of the state capital, Columbia. He would be dressed like Confederate General Robert E Lee and I was to come as Scarlett O'Hara. So, encased in a massive hoop skirt covered by layers of pink tulle and shaded from the sun by a matching parasol, I processed with him to the State Capitol where all the faux Confederate officers and their dates seceded from the American Union. Once at the ball, Bob got drunk and while I sat demurely sipping my Mint Julep, slipped under the table and attempted to grope under my hoop skirt. Offended, I flounced off and went home by myself in a taxi.

Aunt Nell's choice was considerably better: bright young Bud Watts, president of his class at Charleston's prestigious Citadel military college. He took me to a graduation ball where, once again in obligatory hoop skirt and tulle, I stood with him in the receiving line along with the college president, General Mark Clark, a four-star hero of World War II. Bud went on to become a Fulbright Scholar, a Lieutenant General and president of the Citadel.

However, my favorite boyfriend was Paul Carr, a handsome fellow UNC student. Opting not to join a fraternity, he was thoughtful, fun and shared my interest in politics, social issues and literature. I saw him as a future crusading politician or lobbyist for worthwhile causes, so, after he encouraged me to read one of his favorite books, *Elmer Gantry*, Sinclair Lewis' powerful novel about a flamboyant con man who's a shameless Christian minister, I was surprised to discover he planned to go into the Methodist ministry. It became increasingly obvious to us both that I was ill-equipped to be the wife of a Methodist minister and, a few years after graduation, he found his ideal life-partner.

Our 1958 senior year ended with a dramatic graduation ceremony in the university stadium followed by outdoor concerts by the likes of Louis Armstrong and the Modern Jazz Quartet. Then, most of my fellow journalism graduates set out to find jobs. Instead, using the small sums I had earned teaching crafts in summer youth camps plus a generous handout from my parents, I joined a European-bound tour that the fellow student graduates and I were assured would be a cut

above the usual. That's because we would be led by Mr Schotz, the German-American Quaker head of the campus YMCA who not only had worked in Berlin following World War II, but would be placing us with the families of German students when we reached Berlin.

Off with Paul Carr to a UNC party

Later partial newspaper coverage of my time in Berlin

28 Richmond News Leader, Thursday, Dec. 5, 1958

A HOUSE DIVIDED

Situation in Berlin Viewed by Reporter

By MARY MOORE MASON

Berlin is a house divided that has stood. The overwhelming question in today's news is this: can the house be reunited without becoming a pawn of the Soviet Union?

As I flew into Berlin a few months ago I thought, not for the first-time, that the Berlin of two completely different facades was probably an exaggeration. There beneath us stretched the vast city with little difference to be seen when the stewardess announced, "We are now passing from East into West Berlin."

But the differences in the two zones was one to be discovered from the firm reality of the ground and not the air.

(Editor's Note: Mary Moore Mason, News Leader staff writer, recently returned from an extended tour of Europe, including a two-week seminar in Berlin.)

different in the two German "justice" states. Lothar Fisher, a refugee to East German "justice" st it this way: "In the West you are considered innocent until you are proven guilty. In Germany I escaped from are considered guilty until can prove that you are cent."

The experiences of same young man, who is tened to 10 years in

Miss Mason

A Life-Changing Tour Of Europe

Although our transatlantic liner was called the *Italia*, most of our fellow passengers were Bavarian-Americans headed on holiday to their homeland. Soon they were emerging from their cabins dressed in lederhosen, turning the bar into a floating *hofbrauhaus* and leading us all into rollicking German drinking songs. Remaining aloof from them was one of their more elegant countrymen who looked rather like the Italian heart-throb actor Marcello Mastroianni. Introducing himself as a baron, he took a shine to three of us, offering to show us around "his Hamburg".

Soon after we disembarked, he bundled me, Gary, a gay artist, and a tall, blond basketball player named Bob into his car and headed for the Reeperbahn where we had drinks in a bar furnished with booths equipped with telephones so you could invite a stranger across the room to dance … or more. The next attraction was a performance of semi-nude female mud wrestling and the evening ended with a stroll through the streets of the Red Light District. We vowed not to tell Mr Schotz how we had spent our first evening in Europe.

When we reached Berlin I was housed with a kindly German widow who delegated her student daughter, Elsa, to look after me but, in fact, I ended up looking after Elsa. Most days, after mingling with the various German hosts and doing a bit of sightseeing, we headed for the lively West Berlin restaurants and bars where Elsa, unaccustomed to such jolly student life, got quite tipsy. After taking her home by expensive cab, I would smuggle her past her mother, proclaiming what a superb job she had done chaperoning me.

The stand-out to me among the German students was good-looking blond Herbert Kraus who, after telling me how much he loved American jazz, invited me to accompany him to purchase some vintage records in East Berlin. Arriving at the agreed S-bahn station, I found him leaning against a lamp-post, swathed against the damp fog in a turned-up collar trench coat and smoking a cigarette. My heart flipped … I could almost hear background music from Carol Reed's atmospheric *Third Man* film. We found Herbert's elderly record vendor trading by candlelight in the basement of a bombed-out building, then easily returned to West Berlin – this was two years before the Berlin wall went up.

Later, Herbert introduced me to a friend who had escaped from his small East German town with only the clothes he was wearing and a small bag of possessions. With him was his sweetheart, beautiful, dark-haired Marina and this was to be their last week together – as he was penniless, her wealthy industrialist father had insisted she marry the prosperous son of one of his business associates.

Meanwhile, we American students were able to compare the relative gaiety of West Berlin with the regimentation of East Berlin by visiting a Communist youth camp and viewing a menacing military parade before we moved on to Austria, Switzerland, Italy, France and Great Britain, learning more about their cultures, charm and challenges along the way. Our time in Italy was particularly memorable as Mr Schotz arranged for us to spend an evening with a group of Italian students in Florence and, on another evening, one of our group hired a boat to take some of us on a moonlight cruise down the Adriatic – I can still remember the magical sound of *Volare*, then one of Europe's most popular songs, resounding across the water from the candlelit cafes along the shore.

When we got to London, Gary, Bob and I decided to rent a car and head for Scotland, which I considered my ancestral homeland. After enjoying alluring Edinburgh and tough but impressive Glasgow we arrived at Fort William in the western Highlands to discover we were running out of money. "Why don't we all pretend to be Scottish American," I suggested. "Then perhaps someone will offer us a place to stay and some meals."

At first it worked like a charm. Hearing our tale of financial woe, the proprietress of the tea house we stopped at invited us to spend the night and have dinner with her family. But, alas, I didn't leave well enough alone. Remembering the song we sang at school, I replied. "Ah, that is so wonderful as we are all so proud to be Campbells," at which point I burst into song … "The Campbells are coming … Tarah, Tarah!" Suddenly the mood darkened; our new friend, announcing that she just recalled the family had house guests that night, flipped the door's sign from *Open* to *Closed*, ushered us out of the teahouse and strode off up the street.

Astounded, we drove in shock through several villages and then stopped at a roadside pub to recuperate. When I told the barman of our experience – to the great merriment of all those in the pub – he responded: "Ah lassie, have ye not heard of the Massacre of Glencoe near Fort William? The Campbells came there in the dead of winter, took advantage of the hospitality of the MacDonalds and then killed them all, even the babes. Is there any reason why they would want to welcome Campbells to their homes?" Then, when we revealed we weren't really Campbells, one of the kindly villagers offered us shelter for the night while another treated us to dinner.

The Only Woman in a
Southern Newsroom

Returning from Europe older and a bit wiser, it was time to look for a job. Remembering an offer to help with job searches made by the journalism school's dean, Norval Neil Luxon, I hopped into my little red Ford Fiesta and headed for UNC. My timing was perfect, said the dean: *The Charlotte Observer* was at that moment looking for a new reporter for its Woman's Page.

"But I don't want to work on a Woman's Page!" I protested. "Then why did you come to journalism school?" countered the dean. "Certainly not to write about flower arranging, weddings and debutante balls," I sputtered. "Well then, you might have to take a job on one of those weekly newspapers up in the mountains," he said. "They are always desperate for staff and will take anyone."

The phone in his office rang and he apologized: "Sorry, this call was prearranged. It's from *The Richmond News Leader*. They're looking for recent journalism graduates." "Tell them about me!" I kept mouthing, pointing at myself. Putting his hand over the phone mouthpiece, he replied: "Don't be ridiculous! They haven't hired a woman, except on the Woman's Page, since World War II, when they had to because the men went to war."

Extremely cross, I got back in my car and the next day headed for Richmond, seldom visited before as it was about a four-hour drive across the state from Roanoke. Arriving at the downtown office shared by the evening *News Leader* and its sister morning paper, *The Times Dispatch*, I bluffed my way past the guardian of the newsroom, claiming that Dean Luxon had sent me. Upon entering the office of the middle-aged managing editor, Colonel Charles Henry Hamilton, I was greeted courteously, offered a seat and told: "Unfortunately, Miss Mason, there are no openings on the

Woman's Page at the moment but we will certainly let you know when something opens up." When I explained it was not the Woman's Page I was after, he added: "Ah, but there is no place in the newsroom for a charming young Southern lady like you."

"But Colonel Hamilton, "I replied, "I am not a Southern lady and you are not a Southern gentleman. A Southern lady wouldn't

THE RICHMOND NEWS LEADER
RICHMOND, VIRGINIA

CHARLES H. HAMILTON
MANAGING EDITOR

October 10, 1958

Miss Mary Moore Mason,
2736 Stephenson Ave., S. W.,
Roanoke, Va.

Dear Miss Mason:

I am writing in the thought that you might be interested in a position in our news department as an editorial assistant. This is a new category that we have put into effect just this year. It means that you would be working as an assistant to the city editor, doing all sorts of city desk chores and doing a certain amount of writing. The idea back of the classification is that it would lead to graduation into a full reporting job. It is, frankly, something of an experiment, but we have reason to think it will work out well for all concerned. If you are interested in this job, the starting salary would be $56 a week with raises every six months.

Please let me hear from you as soon as possible. You could begin immediately.

Sincerely yours,

C. H. Hamilton,
Managing Editor.

CHH:JS

eavesdrop like I did yesterday on Dean Luxon's phone conversation with you, and a Southern gentleman wouldn't lie to a Southern lady like you just did, claiming there is no place in the newsroom when you told Dean Luxon yesterday there was."

Lost for words and looking for back-up, the Colonel summoned in the courtly news editor, John Leard, who asked: "Do you have any examples of your writing?" at which I produced several features including interviews with celebrity visitors to UNC plus a lengthy Berlin feature I'd written for the Roanoke newspaper. Two weeks later I received a letter hiring me as an editorial assistant at half the salary of one of my UNC male classmates already in the newsroom, but at least it was a foot in the door.

Both *The Times Dispatch* and the *The News Leader* had considerable prestige; the morning paper because its editor, Virginius Dabney, had won a Pulitzer Prize for his stance against the vote-limiting Virginia poll tax, and the evening paper because its previous editor, Douglas Southall Freeman, had won Pulitzer Prizes for his biographies of Robert E Lee and George Washington. Its current editor, James Jackson Kilpatrick, was an

Richmond's Monument Avenue Robert E Lee statue, its base covered by graffiti, is expected to be removed (Photo: Sue Williams)

Richmond - Past Glory, Present Challenges

Richmond, founded in 1736, received its name from the perceived similarity of its hilltop view over the James River to that of Richmond, Surrey, over the River Thames. Graced by a handsome State Capitol designed by Thomas Jefferson, it has enjoyed both the cachet and, more recently, the curse of being the Capital of the Confederacy during what some Southern Americans still refer to as "The War of Northern Aggression". This legacy is remembered by the White House of the Confederacy, occupied during the war by Confederate President Jefferson Davis, the Museum of the Civil War and grand Monument Avenue, its central parkland occupied for decades by statues of Jeff Davis and Confederate military heroes. Then, in the summer of 2020, perceived as symbols of slavery, they were either forcibly or legally removed. As we went to press only two remained: that of Confederate Commander in Chief Robert E Lee, awaiting a legal decision about his future, its base lurid with multi-colored graffiti, and the one dedicated to Richmond-born, African-American tennis champion Arthur Ashe.

outspoken advocate for racial segregation, as was Colonel Hamilton. I, on the other hand, was now going to racially-integrated parties organized by Byron Fielding, an Associated Press friend from the north, and to black nightclubs with a young lawyer friend, Ted Maeder.

Although I had mixed feelings about the affable but hyper-conservative Colonel Hamilton – particularly after he rejected my feature on the plight of the black families in the community – I quite liked Kilpatrick, in spite of our political differences. Not only was he smart, witty and very articulate – he regularly appeared as the conservative spokesman on the nationwide *60 Minutes* TV program – but he also had supported the cause of an African-

American who had been wrongly accused of killing a white policeman, and he had established the "Beatle Bumble Fund". This was dedicated to rewarding those he felt were victims of unjust legal decisions or petty bureaucracy. For instance, when a Virginia public library decided to remove from its shelves all copies of *To Kill a Mockingbird*, which involved the unjust trial of an innocent black man, the Beatle Bumble Fund bought copies, which were then distributed free to anyone who wanted to read them.

My first job was as a copy-taker, typing up stories phoned in by journalists out on the road. This involved three sheets of carbon paper; the original went to the news desk, the first copy to the copy reader's desk, the second to the Associated Press in the neighboring office and the third to the affiliated TV station across the street. I had only been there a few days when a big, hold-the-front-page story came in about a woman giving birth to quadruplets in the local hospital. Alas, I put the carbons in backwards causing an uproar in the office ("that's what comes from hiring a ditsy woman," sneered the police reporter). Handing the top copy to the news desk, I called out "Anyone in the office have a pocket mirror? No? Well, as a woman I do and if someone would hold it for me, I can read the carbon copy correctly and retype the info."

The only woman in The Richmond News Leader *newsroom*

I graduated to becoming the religious news editor, which primarily consisted of taking down details of the schedules of local Sunday church services to be published each Saturday. However, I discovered a wealth of stories – not all of them appeared in the paper – about how the Episcopalian society ladies tried their skills at talking in tongues while holding Tupperware parties; a newly-built church was slowly sinking into quicksand; the lonely local Armenian Orthodox priest was searching for a wife; and a major TV evangelist was claiming you could be healed by placing a "healing rag" on your TV set while you watched him preach on screen.

Now achieving equal pay after threatening to freelance for the *Times Dispatch*, I was officially declared a reporter and moved on to military news, which was meant to merely regurgitate information sent from the various military bases. Instead, I went for first-hand source material and on one occasion got stranded in a snowstorm overnight on a Marine base.

As a keen amateur artist, I particularly enjoyed reviewing the special exhibitions and interviewing the guest artists – some of them quite famous – at the outstanding Virginia Museum of Fine Arts. Other assignments included covering the police courts, talking to the distraught families of people who had been mowed down in a small town by a gunman and, with the aid of the political reporter, investigating a story about the ineptitude of the Red Cross in setting up what was perceived to be a nuclear-threat, early-warning system – that story was picked up by the Associated Press.

Meanwhile, Virginia's controversial anti-integration program known as Massive Resistance was attracting unfavorable national and international publicity. This was particularly true when, in 1959, Prince Edward County closed down its entire public school system for five years rather than allow black and white children to attend the same school. Education for white children was funded in various ways; black children were cast adrift, so when I was sent to interview a group of African-American teenagers, they told me how the school they would have attended had been stripped of desks, blackboards, books and all other teaching materials while a well-equipped and staffed, all-white private school opened up nearby.

The newsroom team I had joined ranged from some quite scholarly Southern gents to the rambunctious police reporter and the raunchy sports editor who, after deadlines passed, crouched down over his desk, phoned his mistress and in a stentorian whisper entreated: "Talk dirty to me, baby!" And, on the other side of a glass wall, there were the Woman's Page ladies who were overseen by the impressive Sylvia Costin. Among them was the delightful, witty Rose Bennett (later Gilbert) who was not only an excellent journalist but also became an amusing travel companion and a lifelong friend.

Some of the other ladies were not so professional. I recall the day when one of their number, Mary Stuart, was sent a syndicated service feature about how you could enhance your old handbags by covering them with linen embroidered with illustrations of kittens and flowers. All she had to do was provide a headline which came out (much to the delight of the sports editor) as *Pretty Pussies Enhance Old Bags*.

When Sylvia returned to the office from a meeting, it was too late to stop the press so she took a hammer and smashed the offending headline on the metal plate as it went round on the printer. Mary Stuart could never understand why the headline was so badly smudged and went on to produce at least one other memorable headline: *Local Women Fidget Over Lengthy Digits*, inspired by the concern Richmond ladies allegedly had when long-distance phone calls done through operators were replaced by direct dialing.

The Kennedy and Nixon Connections

Among my most challenging and yet interesting roles at *The News Leader* was covering the local and state medical, health and welfare beats, so I found myself writing articles about conditions in the prisons and mental hospitals, new developments at the large local hospital and even flying through a terrifying sleet storm in a small plane piloted by an eye surgeon to meet a patient who needed urgent attention. Then, on November 22, 1963, a photographer and I headed off on an assignment to cover a southern Virginia polio epidemic, which was to end in a most unexpected way.

Arriving at a small rural school where the polio-preventing vaccine was to be issued on sugar cubes, we were confronted by a truckload of sobbing black farm workers. "They done shot our president, they done shot our president," they kept wailing. And when we went into the school and turned on the small black-and-white TV, there was the horrifying news that President Kennedy had been shot and killed while participating in a Dallas, Texas motorcade.

"We've got to call the office," I said to the photographer, and when I got the news desk on the phone, I asked if anyone had thought to talk

The Kennedys in the doomed Dallas motorcade (Photo: The New York Times)

to the Kennedys' neighbors at their rural retreat in Fauquier County, northern Virginia. "You do it," was the response, "drop the photographer off in Richmond, take the car and have a story back to us by early tomorrow morning."

Luckily, we had a local newspaper "stringer" in posh Middleburg, near the Kennedys' weekend retreat. He booked a hotel room for me and organized a dinner party with local people who knew the Kennedys, on the assumption that they would provide the ideal tributary quotes. When I sat down to dinner surrounded by local hunt club aristocrats, I discovered to my alarm that they all disliked John Kennedy and were rather glad he was dead.

"He was a jumped-up Catholic with a corrupt father," said one, adding that he and his friends considered JFK an opportunist who had tried to achieve status by marrying into a well-respected local family. Furthermore, "Unlike Jackie, a skilled equestrian, that man would never get on a horse," grumbled one of the guests. Appalled, I pointed out that riding in hunt meets was hardly top priority for a man in constant pain from lifelong spinal problems, intensified by a back injury sustained in World War II. Furthermore, Jackie Kennedy's dad, "Black Jack" Bouvier, was hardly a paragon among men.

Obviously overstaying my welcome, I left without a story – at least not one that could be published in those days. Luckily, later I was able to get fond quotes from the family priest and from neighbors whose children had played with the Kennedy children, meeting my deadline and seeing my story picked up by the Associated Press.

As for my personal life, soon after arriving in Richmond I'd moved into an apartment in the historic Fan District – so called because the streets fan out from small parks. My room mates were three lively and interesting young women. Morag Williamson, from a small town outside Blackpool on England's west coast, had a splendid English accent, a great sense of humor and was apparently a bit of a romantic risk-taker. While on a train in Germany she had met and fallen for a Virginian who invited her to accompany him back to Richmond. However, after spending more time with him, she decided it was not a happily-ever-after situation but stayed on in Richmond anyway.

Danute Dulys, slightly older than the rest of us, had fled with her family from Lithuania during World War II, settled in Baltimore, where she helped support her family by working in a bank and was now a mature art student at Richmond Polytechnic Institute (RPI). Elf-like and crowned by a mane of unruly hair, she had turned her room, entered through a curtain of beads, into an artistic retreat where she did art work and wove on a loom. Elegant, dark-haired Lynn from New England had recently arrived back from a year at the Sorbonne University in Paris and was also studying at RPI.

Soon the apartment became a hub for a diverse group of friends: my Jewish Associated Press buddy, Byron, who gave me a Siamese cat named George Gordon Lord Byron (or George for short) who, on a golden leash, sometimes accompanied me to parties; Ian, a young British doctor; Bob Burrus and Bill Christian, two bright young lawyers; fellow *News Leader* journalist Rose Bennett and the glamorous Gonzalee Ford, then hosting a youth program on local TV as part of her job as the Youth Coordinator for the posh Richmond department store, Thalhimers.

I was particularly impressed when she joined a Civil Rights sit-down with 34 students from the local all-black Virginia Union University at the previously-segregated Thalhimers lunch counter. She told me she was sure she would be fired when she was called to Mr Thalhimer's office; instead "He said he was proud of me".

At the time, Gonzalee was going out with a fellow *News Leader* journalist, Ted Shepherd, who was so tall she claimed she could only communicate with him by walkie talkie. One evening they were queuing up at the movie theater behind another couple when she noticed Ted's fly was unzipped. Alerted, he quickly made himself decent, unaware that in the process he had zipped up the long hair of the woman in front of him. When she turned off the aisle to take her seat and her hair was yanked she screamed; her date hit Ted, assuming he was exposing himself; and Ted lost his balance and fell over several rows of seats.

I found myself in an equally-embarrassing situation one evening when Morag, aware of her apartment mates' bohemian lifestyle, asked us to evacuate the premises while she entertained some staid British friends of her parents. Accompanied by my doctor friend Ian, I went to a going-away party for a Scottish friend who, unknown to us, had heavily spiked the punch. So, quite tipsy, I was carried home early over Ian's shoulder.

Realizing on the apartment's threshold that I should appear to be sober, I asked Ian to put me down. Then, weaving my way through the living room where Morag was entertaining her parents' friends, I headed for the bathroom, where I slipped and fell into the bathtub. Alas, it was full of blue dye and curtains which Danute planned to convert into a dress to wear to a friend's wedding. With the special logic induced by alcohol, I concluded that if I took the path back through the living room to my bedroom and was extremely polite, no one would notice my plight. So covered with curtains and dye, I curtsied, smiled and welcomed the visitors to America as I passed through their midst, waking up the next morning both physically and emotionally blue. Somehow, Morag forgave me.

Along the way, I had taken a splendid trip to Quebec with Rose in her new Volkswagen Beetle – but only after we promised her father that, for safety reasons, one of us would disguise herself as a man if we drove at night. So, each evening we flipped a coin to see which one of us would forego makeup, tuck their hair up and put on a man's hat.

Gonzalee, another friend and I had hitch-hiked around Jamaica, and then I decided to holiday in the Bahamas with aristocratic Austrian Ingrid, who was interning in Richmond with a business contact of her industrialist father.

Lying on the beach in Nassau two days after our arrival in 1963, we were approached by a tall, dark-haired man in a tropical shirt who, snuffing out his cigar in the sand with one of his two-toned shoes, said in a New Jersey accent: "Da Boss sent me over here to ask if yous goils would like to have lunch with him."

"Certainly not!" snapped Ingrid. "Who's da boss?" I asked, and, gesticulating to a slim man in sun glasses and a panama hat seated on a bamboo chair shaded by a beach umbrella, our hospitality courier replied: "Mr Hartford, Huntington Hartford." Knowing Hartford to be one of America's wealthiest men, heir to the USA's largest grocery chain (A&P), and a supporter of the arts, I said: "Certainly ... when and where?", to be told we would be picked up an hour later by private yacht and taken to Mr Hartford's private estate on nearby Paradise Island.

With a reluctant Ingrid in tow, we arrived at the mansion to find seated at the outdoor dining table, Hartford, his current actress wife, who I learned had appeared in some James Bond films, a rather glum Richard Nixon and the former US vice-president's Cuban-American friend Bebe Rebozo. When it was discovered that I was a journalist I was emphatically told not to ask any questions, and, in any case, the lunch was off the record. Most of the conversation was divided between Hartford's plans to convert the surrounding island into his personal fiefdom and commiserations over Nixon's loss of the California governor's race the year before.

After touring the island, Ingrid and I were persuaded to stay for an early dinner, where we were joined by the man from the beach, whose name I have now forgotten, and his wife, a New York showgirl dressed in fetching pea-green toreador pants, her blonde hair swept up in a beehive.

As her hubby made emphatic points by stubbing out his cigar in the butter pats, she enthused over the cocker spaniel that had wandered into the room. "Do you like little doggies, Mr Nixon?" she asked, obviously oblivious of the fact that Nixon's own beloved cocker spaniel, Checkers, given to him by a supporter, had become known throughout the land in 1952 after the then US vice-presidential candidate, accused of taking bribes, had appeared with him on TV.

I became uncomfortable as Hartford and his colleagues kept referring to Nixon as "Dickie boy", suggesting they could help to get him back into power (in 1969 he became US President) and then, after Nixon adjourned himself, suggesting we all go skinny dipping in the sea. Sensing that escape lay with Bebe, I said, "I'm getting bored ... let's go into Nassau and do some clubbing." As soon as the yacht hit shore, Ingrid and I leapt off, shouted thanks and fled back to our modest B&B.

Montmartre, my new home in Paris
(Photo: Heradeus Krifikas/Shutterstock)

A Tale of Two Cities: Paris and Athens

Later, my apartment mate Lynn invited me to accompany her to Paris, where she planned a romantic reunion with her Sicilian-American boyfriend, Sonny Montagna. While there, a summer romance evolved between me and Sonny's quite-charming Parisian friend, Jean-Pierre Jerabek. Keeping in touch with him over a couple of years and feeling it was time for me to move on, I gave in my notice to the newspaper, said a fond farewell to my friends and family and bought a one-way ticket to France. By coincidence, Lynn, having ended her romance with Sonny, was on the same flight, headed to Paris on honeymoon with her new husband, Eric.

Although Jean-Pierre, who lived in a cozy apartment over a carpenter's shop in Montmartre, urged me to move in with him, I opted for independence, settling down in the nearby, seedy Hotel Terminus. My room, tucked away in the eaves and reached by a long, winding staircase, was enhanced by a wash-basin, bidet and fading floral wallpaper. There was a shared toilet nearby but no usable bathtub. The rather tyrannical concierge had locked it up after filling the tub with the possessions of a student tenant who had scampered without paying his rent.

So, adorned in numerous layers of clothing and carrying a large plastic bag and a bar of soap, I trudged down the steep hill to the public baths, washing both my laundry and myself as I stripped down layer by layer. Discovering that the male attendant had drilled peep holes in the shower, I took to plugging them with chewing gum. Then I would trudge back up the hill with my heavy load of wet laundry, which was then hung from a rope stretched across the room, the water dripping on plastic bags strewn across the floor.

Soon after my arrival, Jean-Pierre announced that as a special treat he had invited French friends to an American dinner, which I would provide. Quite concerned as I had never learned how to cook and my schoolgirl French was quite faulty, I ended up producing devilled eggs, which the guests had never seen before, hot dogs with all the fixings and strawberry shortcake. They all professed to find the meal delicious, although I had my doubts that it lived up to their expectations.

On weekends, Jean-Pierre showed me around the enchanting city and on many weekdays I visited his mother – in reality his aunt, who had married his father when his mother died. Always dressed in black but with a warm smile, she was helping me improve my French, a bit complicated as she professed to speak no English. To solve the problem, I began purchasing my favorite American novels in French. She would then read them and we would endeavor to discuss them in her native language – a particular challenge when I tried to explain the special relationships that Southern girls sometimes have both with their fathers and the family's black help as revealed in William Styron's Virginia-set novel *Lie Down in Darkness*. Meanwhile, Sonny was showing me around Paris, sometimes in thrilling rides on the back of his motorcycle.

As time progressed, both Jean-Pierre and I realized that, as special as our summer romance had been, it was not destined to last, so I decided to move on. The question was where. As Sonny was headed for a job interview in Geneva, he suggested I accompany him while I made up my mind. He emerged from his meeting with Bernie Cornfeld, the Turkish-born, Brooklyn-bred owner of Investors Overseas Services, with a job selling mutual funds to Greek sea captains, and I decided to accompany him to Athens.

Posing as a couple, we soon secured a nice modern apartment close to Syntagma Square and I headed off to obtain information from the Greek tourism office. Learning that I was a former journalist from the USA, the quite charming director made me an offer: he needed English language tourism information and press releases, how would I like to produce them? There was, alas, no

With Sonny Montagna in Greece

money but he could arrange for me to enjoy free hospitality throughout the country as I researched the material.

Sometimes I accompanied a jolly group of Greek journalists, all of whom spoke some English while I picked up a few helpful Greek phrases. More often, I set off by car with Sonny, by now my romantic partner, traveling as far south as the Peloponnese's Mani Peninsula and as far north as Greece's second-largest city, Thessaloniki. Or we dropped the car at Piraeus and took a ferry to whichever island took our fancy. Particularly magical were Mykonos during the Greek Orthodox Easter celebrations and Crete, where we walked for miles after the local bus broke down, ending up at a small fishing village called Matala.

Basing ourselves in a tiny, rustic guest house there, we hiked through the Cretan hills filled with foraging goats, watched the night fishermen in their lantern-lit boats and explored the cliff-side caves with their ancient burial sites. Then we headed for the local taverna to join the ouzo- and retsina-drinking locals who, if the village's one telephone rang, would crowd around it, hoping to pick up and relay gossip from other villages on the party line. Somehow, it felt like *Brigadoon*, destined to disappear for another century when we departed. Instead, it appeared on the cover of *Life* magazine in July 1968 as the latest spot discovered – and probably destroyed by – swarms of hippies.

Back in Athens, Sonny, his Italian-American colleague Steve Zalenga and I would join the sea captains and their wives for dinner. The men loved such ribald humor as seating unsuspecting guests on fart cushions and the women were often drama queens. One night in a waterfront restaurant, one stood up mid-meal, a wine glass in hand and toasted we three Americans with the following words: "Why is it that the food in all American restaurants is so terrible?" Rising to the occasion, I stood up, glass in hand, and replied: "Because, madam, all the restaurants are run by Greeks." Surprisingly all our hosts, except madam, roared with laugher and there was much noisy bouncing up and down on the fart cushions.

On another evening it was decided that I should relax in Steve's waterfront hotel while he and Sonny went off on a mutual fund-selling mission. Given the key to Steve's room by the desk clerk and

---

Athens in the Mid–1960s

It was a great time to be in Athens, partly because of two great films that were then putting modern Greece on the international map. In the 1960 film *Never on Sunday,* free-spirited lady of easy virtue Ilya, portrayed by Greek actress Melina Mercouri, livened up the life of stuffy American tourist Homer (Jules Dassin). Its catchy title song and exuberant bouzouki music won the 1960 Oscar and Mercouri was chosen best actress at the Cannes Film Festival. Then, in 1964, came *Zorba the Greek,* set in Crete and starring Anthony Quinn as the irrepressible peasant Zorba. Soon we, like Zorba, were dancing the sirtaki on the beach, in tavernas and other public places. Alas, it was all to end in 1967 when the right-wing colonels staged a coup and took over the country for seven years.

knowing they would be gone for some time, I stripped off to my undies, slipped into bed and was in a deep sleep when I awoke to the sound of a key in the door. And there was a large Greek man obviously overjoyed to see me. (Piraeus was known for its ladies of easy virtue.)

Alarmed, I leapt from the bed, swathed in a sheet and stumbled around the room and out into the hall, playfully chased by my new admirer. Luckily, at that moment Sonny and Steve appeared in search of me – I had obviously been given a key to the wrong room. Baffled, my new Greek admirer retreated to his room accompanied by the three of us. And while I put my clothes back on Steve and Sonny sold him a mutual fund.

Where Are They Now?

Jean-Pierre remained in Paris, married a French lady, had children and, when we got back in touch by mail years later, told me I would be alarmed to see him as he now "looked like a crocodile". Surely not! Sonny married a Dutch air hostess but we then lost touch. Tried and later acquitted for financial mismanagement, Bernie Cornfeld based himself in Los Angeles, where he lived in a mansion once leased by Hollywood star Douglas Fairbanks and hobnobbed with the likes of Elizabeth Taylor, Warren Beatty and Tony Curtis.

During all this day-to-day frivolity I not only produced English features for my friend in the Greek tourist board but also began to sell travel stories to some American and British newspapers. However, my money was beginning to run out, my parents had summoned me to Paris, where they were soon due on holiday and, once again, it was time for me to move on.

Alas, my suitcase had long since fallen apart so I arrived in Paris not only rumpled from my long train journey but also with all my belongings in a large cardboard box, tied by dirty cord. Greeting me in the lobby of the grand Hotel Meurice, my father was obviously unimpressed. Nudging my improvised suitcase across the lobby with his foot he muttered: "I can never understand why you left a good secure job in Virginia to get involved with a Frenchman and then ended up a hippy in Greece." Although my mother was obviously much more sympathetic, the strain of it all – or perhaps the magnificent view – caused her to burst into tears at the top of the Eiffel Tower.

After I adamantly refused to return with them to the USA, my father finally suggested: "Well if you are determined to stay here why don't you go somewhere civilized like England where they at least speak English," and my mother chipped in: "Why don't you call that nice friend of yours, Morag? She's now living back in England and seems like a very sensible lady. Maybe you could stay for awhile with her!"

Punting past Cambridge University along the River Cam
(Photo: iGiacomo Ferroni /unsplash)

A New Life – and Job – in England

"Great news!" responded Morag over the phone. "You can stay at my place near Cambridge and then look for a job in London." So, endowed with some funds from my long-suffering parents, I headed off to England, where I found Morag, not unexpectedly, enjoying a lively lifestyle. Working in Cambridge and living in a picturesque thatched cottage in the nearby village of Meldreth, she welcomed me with a costume party where, memorably, one of the taller male guests, dyed green to represent a sinister pagan god, left emerald hand-prints all along the low ceiling.

I felt lucky to be under the wing of such a sophisticated, well-connected lady as we explored the East Anglian countryside and I met her friends. Among them was a Cambridge University student who invited her to the legendary May Ball. As his rather lacklustre friend had been stood up by his date, I was enlisted to replace her and we were soon traipsing from one ancient college to the next listening to live bands, sipping Pimms and dining on swan and roast suckling pig. Joining us along the way was an elegant

young woman in a long, flowing gown who could have stepped out of a pre-Raphaelite painting.

The daughter of a baroness and the wife of artist and gallery-owner John Dunbar, she was Marianne Faithfull, who later became a Swinging Sixties icon, girlfriend of Mick Jagger and an acclaimed singer and actress.

Morag Williamson (later Hann), welcomed me to England

Heading off job-hunting to London, I took a room in a Marble Arch area flat already occupied by no-nonsense Sheila from Northern Ireland, jolly Beth from Australia and Norah, a "resting" Scottish actress who had most recently appeared as one of the three witches in a regional production of *Macbeth*. The flat was extremely cold – particularly if you ran out of shillings to feed the wall meter – so we all slept with hot water bottles to the sound of the drip-drip-drip of wet laundry hanging from the clothes lines in our shared bathroom.

The first advert I answered in *The Times* was for a PR for the Church of England and I was invited for a job interview in offices near Westminster Abbey on the basis that I had been the religious news editor of an American newspaper. The interview went smoothly until I explained that my job had involved researching and writing stories about how Billy Graham took Elizabeth Taylor to task for her multi-married lifestyle; Daddy Grace, a black evangelist, took a dunking after promising to walk on water in South Carolina's Pee Dee River; and Master X, another evangelist with access to an ancient airplane, made a living flying men's semen "up into the stratosphere" where, he claimed, it received a blessing of fertility from a benevolent God.

Then I picked up a large, glossy magazine entitled *International,* noticed it was primarily about travel and dropped by its New Bond Street office. Would they be interested in some travel articles about Greece? I asked the editor, Nicholas Guppy. His response was "no" to Greece, but "yes" to the USA as there were so few travel writers in London who had traveled beyond the main gateway cities, whereas I had journeyed extensively to places such as the Carolinas, Texas and the Rocky Mountains.

So I joined the small staff and began editing copy from a quite varied range of contributors: an adventurous lord who had been a World War II fighter pilot and now specialized in writing about obscure places; another chap who was an expert on mountain gorillas; and a quite pretentious peeress whom I shall call Lady Be Bad who wrote primarily about posh resorts and destinations.

Our designer was a young (later Sir) Terence Conran, who went on to found the Habitat furniture empire. After hearing me complain endlessly about London barmen's inability to produce a good dry Martini, he bought all the relevant ingredients and invited me to his place to mix them properly. I apparently made them too strong, for after two large cocktails I could not get back down his spiral staircase, threw up all over his spotless white carpet and, according to my very disapproving flatmates, was delivered home comatose, a sign pinned to my blouse that stated: "So you know how to mix a good Dry Martini!"

Nicholas Guppy had quite a remarkable background. Born in Trinidad of aristocratic, Huguenot ancestry – including Sir Frances Dashwood, the creator of the notorious mid-18th-century Hellfire Club, and a grandfather who discovered the tropical fish, now known as the guppy – he was a botanist, explorer, environmentalist and the author of *Wai-Wai*, a colorful account of his time with the indigenous people of British Guiana. His Iranian wife, Shusha, was an acclaimed writer and singer in both Persian and English and his son, Darius, was later to obtain fame as the best man at the wedding of Lord Spencer, Princess Diana's brother, a good friend of the youthful Boris Johnson, and notoriously, the perpetrator of a fake New York jewelry heist and insurance scam that earned him five years in jail.

Meanwhile, I had moved to a townhouse on Campden Hill near Notting Hill Gate, which I was sharing with an Australian radio and TV journalist Sandra Harris while my circle of friends was expanding. Among them were Bill Mitchell, a colorful Canadian actor, best known for his deep, gravelly, Oscar Wells-like voice, which gained him a premier place in the then fledgling advertising voice-over market, and Sandy Zane, the deputy press officer for Pan American, then the world's leading airline.

Bill took me to parties and pubs where fellow guests included actors Peter Finch and John Hurt and as Sandy had published a novel soon after graduating from Yale, we ended up at many a celebrity publishing party. Guests included Tom Wolfe, then acclaimed as one of the leaders of the "new journalism" and later author of *The Bonfire of the Vanities*; entertainers Peter Cook and Dudley Moore; and Pierre Salinger, the former press secretary for Presidents Kennedy and Johnson.

Another friend, George, a London-based croupier from Reno, Nevada, gave me his 1949 Triumph Roadster before he decamped to Mexico with a Peace Corps lady. Settling into this photogenic if somewhat-decrepit convertible, I set out, wind blowing through my hair, to explore the English West Country, accompanied by my Scottish actress friend Norah and, in the rumble seat, Paula, a film industry buddy, who looked swell in a large picture hat and pink feather boa.

All went well until we reached a back road somewhere in Dorset where Norah announced the car was on fire. At first I didn't believe her – as an actress she was prone to over dramatize – but then, smelling smoke, I pulled to the side of the road and both Norah and I leapt out while Paula struggled to extract herself. Miraculously, a dog-collared English clergyman suddenly appeared with a large tub of water which he threw over the car and, to her dismay, Paula.

It turned out that the exhaust pipe had fallen off and sparks had lit some of the vehicle's wooden underpinning, a problem soon rectified by a Rastafarian workman at a small garage just up the road. But why, you may ask, was the clergyman on hand with the basin of water? Because he and his wife, retired missionaries, were camping in the nearby field where they were bathing their two adopted African babies.

About this time I began to worry about the future of *International* and, indeed, my own as, without a work permit, I was illegally employed. Sandy, by then my special beau, decided to move back to the USA to take up his old job on the *San Francisco Chronicle*, and, on an impulse I applied for his job at Pan Am. To my delight, I got it and, after a brief visit back to the USA, found a work permit waiting for me at Heathrow Airport.

London - in the Mid-1960s - Swinging or Recuperating?

When I arrived in "Swinging London" in 1965, it was still recuperating from World War II. There were still some bomb-damaged buildings, and we kept warm at night by putting shillings in wall meters or building coal fires – thus contributing to the deep yellow fog, really smog, that blanketed the city on many an evening. Food shops seemed to be mainly stocked with root vegetables, most of the restaurant food was appalling – I had to learn to adapt to mushy peas and picturesquely-named Toad in the Hole and Spotted Dick. And when I was told that "London swings like a pendulum do" I thought "big deal – the Londoners are just doing what we young Americans had been doing all along – partying." But as I became increasingly aware of the vibrant post-war renewal, the break down of the class system, the delightful British sense of humor and the historical and cultural treasure houses all around, I decided that, to paraphrase the immortal words of Doctor Samuel Johnson, "If you are tired of London you are tired of life."

The first transatlantic Boeing 747 "Jumbo Jet" arrives at London's Heathrow (Photo: The Pan Am Historical Museum)

Promoting the First
Transatlantic "Jumbo Jet"

My Pan Am boss, Fred Tupper, proved to be the ideal mentor for someone new in PR and the aviation industry. A London-based New York newspaper correspondent during World War II, he had married an Englishwoman and stayed on to become "The World's Most Experienced Airline's" most experienced overseas PR. As a keen and knowledgeable sports fan, he also covered the Wimbledon tennis matches and various UK golf tournaments for *The New York Times* and when I timidly asked if I could also do some freelance travel writing he said, fine, as long as it didn't interfere with my job at Pan Am.

My fellow workers were interesting and diverse individuals. Fred's and my secretary, Eva Lorant, had fled Hungary with her parents during World War II, and later became one of my son Mark's godmothers; ticket office manager Peter Moss' daughter, Kate, became a super model as did, later, her half-sister, Lottie; and the charming sales manager, Bill Lyons, was later revealed to be the "headless" (unidentifiable) man in the risque photos used by the Duke of Argyll in his notorious 1960's divorce case against his beautiful wife, Margaret. (Apparently she and Bill had been lovers for six years, which explains the mysterious female phone messages that were regularly left at the Pan Am office.)

To learn more about Pan Am, I was sent to Miami to spend a few days at the stewardess training school. Dressed in a multi-patterned mini-culotte outfit and thigh-high purple suede boots, loop earnings dangling from my ears – after all it was the Swinging Sixties back in London! – I slipped into the back of a classroom filled with neatly-coiffed young ladies dressed in trim blue and white uniforms. "I see we have with us Miss Mason from our London office," said the instructor. "Would you please come to the front of the room and turn around, Miss Mason." As I slowly revolved, she said, "Now class, this is definitely not the way a Pan Am lady should dress!" Chastised, I returned to the next class more appropriately attired.

A couple of years later I was asked to advise the press that Pan Am was establishing a stewardess base in London. Deciding to enhance the story, I indicated that there had been a huge demand among the stewardesses to be based in London because they considered English men to be the most desirable in the world. It made front page news.

Then I was sent off on my first press trip, to Istanbul, which included among the media the same grand Lady Be Bad I had dealt with at *International*. As was her custom, she was accompanied by her husband who, despite being a lord, dutifully trotted along behind her like a pet dog. Ensconced in a rather posh Hilton hotel, which she as an "expert on Turkey" had recommended, and focusing on the most magnificent sites of the city, all went well until some of the journalists became restive. Could we not, they suggested, experience some of the nightlife of Istanbul? So, after consultation with the local tourism office, I whisked us off to a nightclub overlooking the Bosphorus and run by, it was said, an elderly former attaché of Mustafa Kemal Ataturk, the founder of modern Turkey.

As the wine flowed, we enjoyed the delicious food – although it was difficult to dine when a sparsely-clothed belly dancer was undulating tabletop amidst the plates. Then a large lady with hennaed hair, dressed in a voluminous white wedding gown, moved to the mic and wailed a song of thwarted love as mascara flowed down her cheeks and gentlemen waltzed together across the ballroom floor. The journalists all loved it, except for Lady Be Bad.

"This is awful, Mary," she hissed. "I shall have to complain to my dear friends Fred Tupper and the Minister of Tourism! Come along, dear." She snapped her fingers and her husband dutifully trotted behind her as she swept out the door. Moments later a beaming Minister of Tourism, surrounded by other officials, joined us. "I was just waiting for Lady Be Bad to leave," he said, "I knew it was not her thing. Now let's have fun!" From this came one of my first travel stories for the *Sunday Telegraph* which, as I recall, began: "As I waltzed by the Bosphorus with Kemal Ataturk's attaché".

Numerous other travel features followed, some for *The Observer* and *The Times* but primarily for *The Sunday Telegraph*, which particularly liked pieces written by a non-Brit about UK destinations. Only one was rejected – an extremely earthy piece describing a northern England working men's club that featured a chorus line of semi-nude men pretending to be coal miners, one of them with a plastic hand jutting out of his fly. "My dear Mary," said travel editor Nigel Buxton, "you must remember that our paper is read by retired wing commanders and vicars."

The American magazines, on the other hand, appeared to be delighted by stories about the eccentricities of the Europeans, the Brits in particular, which were sometimes accompanied by cartoons. Among them was a feature about the jokes Europeans tell about their fellow Europeans.

The Belgians loved to josh the Dutch about their financial "meanness"; the Dutch, the Belgians for what they considered to be stupidity; the British about the feyness of the Irish, and the Irish ... well about the Irish. And that was not to forget the things various Europeans did that irritated others: for the Brits, the list was led by the Italian queue jumpers, and for almost everyone, the Germans' addiction to blocking off all the sun beds and key beach sites at seaside resorts.

Meanwhile, there was a vibrant social life, particularly at the spontaneous gatherings I dubbed Noah's Ark parties as they all appeared to be attended by two of every kind. They were hosted in her Knightsbridge flat by my flamboyant, red-haired American friend Bunny Dexter – one party alone included among its guests Viscount Weymouth (Alexander Thynne to his friends), splendid in a long oriental robe, ribbons in his beard and accompanied by a duo of his reputed 74 "wifelets"; two controversial Labor politicians; two gay novelists; and Anglo-African twins who inexplicitly arrived on roller-skates.

Later, I headed out to visit Alexander in his stately home. The purpose of my visit was to research a story for an American magazine on the gimmicks British aristocrats use to keep their stately homes financially sound. Arriving at Wiltshire's palatial Elizabethan Longleat, I was ushered into the grand wood-paneled library of Alexander's handsome, business suit-attired father, the 6th Marquess of Bath. Offering me a glass of sherry, he recounted how he had brought extra funding to the massive estate by installing lions on the premises, regularly hosting Teddy Bear Picnics and staging such special events as skydiving knights adorned in plastic armor.

Then, with what appeared to be slight hesitation, he offered to pass me on to his son and heir. Barefoot, although it was autumn, and as flamboyantly garbed as when we first met, Alexander warmly welcomed me into his wing of Longleat with a large goblet of red wine. "Do meet my wife," he said fondly, gesturing to a framed photo of his greatly pregnant – and nude – Hungarian actress wife, Anna Gael. Most of the year, he said, she lived in Paris, while his two children resided here at Longleat, well-tended by a nanny.

Escorting me into the nursery, he proudly pointed out the floor-to-ceiling painting he had created of a sinister, witch-like creature. Then we continued into apartments that featured erotic Kama Sutra-inspired murals he had also created, their message enhanced by certain sexual appendages projecting from the wall. There were also portraits up a stairwell of some of my host's various "wifelets", who lived in cottages around the estate – he was sometimes referred to by the media as "The Loins of Longleat".

In fact, at Bunny's party, one of his wifelets, Nola Fontaine, a rather jolly, Jamaica-born cabaret singer, had suggested I join their number; I declined on the basis of not having time to spare in my oh-so-busy schedule.

As I prepared to leave Longleat, Alexander gave me a farewell gift, *The Carry-Cot*, a Gothic novel he had written, which, as I recall, recounted the story of a stately home occupied by, among others, a sinister nanny and a malevolent butler.

(In April 2020, Alexander, age 87, died from Covid-19 and his son and heir, Ceawlin, 8th Marquess of Bath, said he planned to remove Longleat's murals and evict the numerous wifelets. Luckily, Nola did not have to endure that indignity – she predeceased Alexander by five years.)

Alexander Thynne, the 7th Marquess of Bath in his
1926 Daimler outside stately Longleat
(Photo: Barry Batchelor/PA Photos)

Back to Bunny, when she was not inventing such things as *Shrink*, a Monopoly-style board game based on Freudian concepts, she was expounding on how every woman needed three men in her life – Mr Physical, Mr Intellectual and Mr Emotional – and on how she planned to produce an heir via artificial insemination.

At one of her legendary Ladies Lunches held in a Chinese restaurant and attended by only one male – an elegantly dressed, quite posh British gent – Bunny announced, to his obvious surprise, that she had selected him to be the father of her child. Rising to the occasion, he pulled out his pocket diary, perused it and said: "Jolly good, Bunny. Have your secretary call my secretary to set up an appointment." Bunny could never understand why he thereafter didn't respond to her phone calls.

As I headed off to explore Europe, I discovered that a woman traveling on her own often faces unusual challenges. Not long after checking into a small hotel in Madrid, I was invited out for drinks and dinner by a fellow guest, a rather handsome young Italian businessmen named Marco. As we sat sipping cocktails on a grander hotel's roof terrace, he admired my outfit and said: "Your dress is very pretty but I don't remember you wearing that color before." Odd, I thought, as we had just met, and seeing my surprise he explained that I reminded me of someone he once knew.

A day or two later I caught the train to Toledo and was surprised to find him on board. He explained he was en route to visit his sister and her family who had a second home in Toledo and invited me to join them. When we arrived, he introduced me in Italian and suddenly bottles of Prosecco appeared and everyone began toasting both Marco and me.

What nice, friendly folk are the Italians, I thought, and Marco promised to explain more about their warm hospitality after we admired the paintings in the El Greco Museum and returned to Madrid. Inviting me into a dimly-lit taverna after we arrived back in the city, he asked the manageress, a rather blowsy elderly lady with hennaed hair, for a private room as we needed to talk without distraction, and I suddenly found myself in a bedroom with a bolted door. "The family were delighted to hear about our forthcoming marriage," said Marco, "and this time, promise you won't leave me."

"Isn't this a bit sudden?" I protested. "And what do you mean 'this time'?" He explained that the moment he saw me and heard I worked for Pan Am, he realised I was his dead fiancée reincarnated. She had been a Pan Am stewardess who was killed in a tragic road accident three years before.

Oops, I thought ... how do I get out of this one? As he began to undress, I moved swiftly to the balcony and called out: "Come quickly, Marco, you won't believe what has just happened down in the square!" He joined me and as he peered below, I leapt back, shut and locked the French windows, unbolted the bedroom door and fled back to the hotel, locking myself in my room and checking out at dawn the next morning. I hope Marco somehow, someday found his replacement fiancée but she certainly wasn't going to be me.

Heading south, I delighted in Seville's Alcazar and Cathedral but wasn't sure how best to continue on to Granada. Go to the local bar, I was told, and ask for a shared taxi. And, indeed, one was waiting with only one other passenger aboard, a young opera student. As his English was non-existent and I was ill-equipped with schoolgirl Spanish, we were reduced to sharing a bottle of wine and belting out passages from our favorite operas, of course including *Carmen*. And then I discovered he wasn't going to Granada at all but to a family wedding at a sunflower plantation along the way. So I found myself dancing away part of the afternoon with various large, jolly farmers reeking of garlic before continuing on by taxi to my Granada hotel.

After a day spent in the fairytale Alhambra and Generalife Gardens, I was told by the very pleasant middle-aged hotel manager that I must go and watch the gypsies dance before I left the city. In fact, he kindly offered to accompany me to the caves where this took place. Strolling back through a garden some distance from the hotel, I thanked him for the pleasant evening and he replied that we would now be spending the night at his home nearby. Oh damn, I thought, here we go again. Luckily, I found a taxi and fled back to the hotel where I pushed the furniture against the door as it had a faulty lock, ignoring the rattling door knob in the middle of the night. Another dawn check-out when, mercifully, the manager was not on duty.

Meanwhile, it was back to business and what a business it was! Pan Am was due to introduce the first of the "Jumbo Jets" that were set to revolutionize international air travel, and in 1968, I was sent to the Boeing factory near Seattle, Washington, to join other Pan Am PRs from around the world for the unveiling of the amazing Boeing 747, the world's largest aircraft, its tail nearly as tall as a five-storey building, with a length and width that would overwhelm the average football stadium.

Its opulent interior, we were told, could seat as many as 362 passengers but there was still one matter to be resolved: how to utilize the large hump over the cockpit. Reached from First Class via a spiral staircase, should it accommodate more seating, a dining area, a cocktail bar, or, as one of the waggish Pan Am PRs suggested, a honeymoon suite for the likes of the multi-married Elizabeth Taylor? We then continued to the Pratt and Whitney plant in Connecticut to view the most powerful aviation jet engine ever produced.

On January 22, 1970, the first 747 flight arrived from New York in London and Fred and I accompanied a capacity load of media on an "around the rooftops" flight. As I recall, the rather laconic captain announced upon take-off: "Well folks, let's see if we can get this crate up into the air."

Meanwhile, Pan Am was working closely with the entertainment business, including the Disney empire – in return for free flights for some of its staff, we were supposed to have access to some of the Disney characters, including Mickey Mouse, for promotional purposes. However, whenever I phoned the London office, I was stonewalled by the secretary to the relevant executive. Then, one night at a Disney-sponsored event at the US Embassy, I was asked if I would take Mickey Mouse to the ladies room.

When I queried this on gender grounds, I was told that this Mickey was not a he but a she, and none-other than the very stonewalling secretary I had been dealing with.

Knowing that while in costume and in character she was not allowed to talk, I asked her to indicate how badly she needed to go to the "loo" by a nod of the head. And when she responded with furious head bobbing I said: "OK, Mickey Mouse, I will take you on one condition – that you put me through to your boss next time I phone. Otherwise I am walking off and you can stand there and pee in your pants." It worked both to her benefit and mine: her mouse head was removed, the long invisible back zipper released – and thereafter I successfully worked regularly with Mickey Mouse, Goofy, Donald Duck and their cross-species buddies.

James Bond also regularly arrived on Pan Am, the scenes reinforced by flight footage we held in stock. And when Stanley Kubrick's iconic *2001: A Space Odyssey* hit the screens in 1968, its space shuttle and the stewardesses

Was Mickey Mouse really a woman in disguise?

and other crew were all clearly Pan Am. That helped encourage some 93,000 people around the world to sign up for the airline's First Moon Flight Club, which I was then asked to explain to a BBC-TV camera crew while perched on a bar stool in Chelsea's *Man in the Moon* pub.

And speaking of James Bond, one of the parties I was taken to by my actor friend Bill was hosted by a rather obnoxious fellow actor who thought he had been talent-spotted as the next James Bond. When he realized that I was the only person there not indulging in various mind-blowing substances, he took a dislike to me, snatched up the shoes I had removed and threw them out the mews house window into a snow storm.

Both angry and alarmed when I went to the door and couldn't see them, I decided that his resident, but then absent, actress girlfriend must have some suitable footwear. So going into her closet, I selected a knee-high pair of gold leather boots and went home in style. I often wondered how the would-be Agent 007 explained their absence to his girlfriend.

Pan Am particularly liked to promote not only its various American destinations but also their popular culture, particularly music. Thus I was asked to organize a jazz-focused media event featuring Boston-based pianist George Wein, founder of the renowned Newport Jazz Festival, saxophonist Buddy Tate and cornet player Ruby Braff. Among the guests was a tall, dark-haired music photographer named David Redfern.

Discovering that he had been to the Newport Festival, traveled with the Beatles on their famous *Magical Mystery Tour*, loved America and liked American women (he said he'd had a Chicago-based girlfriend who was a fellow photographer), I decided he was my type of guy and we started going out together to places such as Ronnie Scott's jazz club. Then I discovered he was married with two young children and broke off the romance. Later, after he and his wife, Kate, separated, he joined me in my new flat on West London's Holland Park Avenue.

Gradually I became part of his world, attending a private party held for Duke Ellington in an elegant London flat, chatting in the Ronnie Scott's dressing room with delightful Dizzy Gillespie, who I discovered came from the same South Carolina town as one of my uncles, and becoming a lifetime buddy of Meg Walters, the actress wife of one of David's jazz musician friends – at the time she was appearing in the provocative, pioneering production of *Oh! Calcutta!*.

Mary and David Redfern on a writer/photographer assignment

Meanwhile, David began traveling with me not only to the USA but also to such places as Thailand, Japan and Hong Kong. And, in 1974, the Hamlyn Publishing Group commissioned me to write *The Picture Book of the USA,* which included a few of David's photos. Along the way I was also selected as the only airline representative in the British Association of Women in Public Relations.

On one of Pan Am's "Round the World" flights, I was upgraded to First Class, where I found myself seated near the First Lady of the Philippines, Imelda Marcos. At each stop – Frankfurt, Beirut, Istanbul, etc – she would emerge from the upstairs cabin in another dazzling outfit, disembark and be met by some dignitary in a limo with blacked-out windows. Re-boarding, usually with a large bouquet of flowers, she would present these to one of her handmaidens and regally instruct: "Distribute these to the people in economy class." Along the way, she and I became quite chummy; in fact, she invited me to visit her in Manila. It was an invitation I always regretted not following up, if only to see her reputed 1,200 pairs of shoes.

The Dawn of Mass Transatlantic Air Travel

Although the jet age began in the 1950s with the launch of the de Havilland Comets and Boeing 707s, it was the 1970's launch of the Boeing 747 – pioneered by Pan Am – that led to mass transatlantic tourism. Not only could the "Jumbo Jet" carry two-and-a-half times more passengers than the Boeing 737 but the resulting demand for competitively-priced air transport led to deregulation and the launch of numerous new airlines from the USA and other destinations. So it was with sadness that I read while completing this book that British Airways among other airlines was taking its remaining 747s, fondly known as "The Queen of the Skies", out of scheduled commercial service. The reason was not only the economic ravages of the Covid-19 pandemic but also the fact that newer long-haul aircraft were less fuel-hungry and more economically efficient.

One of the key attractions at Space Center Houston is the Boeing 747 which ferried space shuttles

Married Life in Trendy Notting Hill

On one side of the Holland Park Avenue flat that David and I now shared was the home of the prominent Labor politician Wedgwood Benn and his American wife, Caroline. So given was he to humanitarian causes that for a time he allowed a vagrant to live in a small hut in his front garden. On the other side was a prominent Northern Irish TV actor, Jimmy Ellis, then portraying Inspector Bert Lynch in the long-running police drama Z Cars, and his actress wife, Beth, who was destined to be another lifelong friend.

Upstairs from them was a World War II airman who, like the famous Douglas Bader, had lost both legs when his plane was shot down. Remarkably, that did not deter him from running around with women other than his wife. She took to phoning me with this lament: "Mary, he's gone walkabouts again. Do you know where he has gone?" "How would I know," I would patiently respond. "Well, you're in the travel industry, so you should know!" she snapped back.

My downstairs neighbor was a lady journalist whose current beau, made contemplative by the aromatic substance that he frequently smoked, would often sit legs crossed like a Hindu guru in our shared back garden. One night I awoke to a great ruckus to find my neighbor, naked except for a pair of large yellow kitchen gloves chasing a large black bird around the garden. The next day she explained: it had flown through the open French doors and landed on her boyfriend's head at an unfortunate moment, so, not liking to touch it, she sensibly donned the rubber gloves and dealt with the matter.

We also had regular visits from our charlady, Mrs Loveridge, who had a cockney accent as thick and rich as clotted cream and always wore her hat even in the midst of intense cleaning.

Periodically the jolly cockney chimney sweep would appear to pat Mrs Loveridge on her bottom and call her "pet" while diligently stuffing his long cleaning brush up the chimney.

However, Mrs Loveridge's real love was a Polish chef with whom she was living. As she could not pronounce his name, she simply referred to him as 'chef', praising him for gifting her with treasurers that had "fallen off the back of a lorry", in other words, acquired in a dubious manner. Upon going to her bathroom, I found the bathtub filled with jars of pickled onions. "You must particularly like pickled onions," I politely said as I joined her for tea in her sitting room. "Oh, no, madam," was her reply. "But when chef found them they were such a bargain!"

After David and I got married in the rather fashionable Caxton Hall registry office in 1971, followed by a blessing service in the chapel of St Bride's, "the journalists' church" just off Fleet Street, we held our reception at Park Lane's grand Dorchester Hotel. Learning that we were not due to go on honeymoon for quite some time, the Dorchester's gracious PR lady, Marjorie Lee, suggested that we spend that evening *gratis* in the hotel's Harlequin Suite. It was the favorite London base for Hollywood superstar Elizabeth Taylor.

The reception over, and accompanied by a number of close friends, we traipsed up an internal spiral staircase to view our overnight accommodation. The shiny, vivid wallpaper was patterned with diamond shapes and there was a huge canopied

bed, a mirrored ceiling and a pink marble bathroom installed at the request of Ms Taylor.

Welcome from the Dorchester Hotel (Photo: The Dorchester Hotel)

Oddly enough, there was a second small adjoining bedroom. "Probably a waiting room for Elizabeth's next husband," quipped one of our guests.

A butler suddenly appeared and asked: "How many of you will be dining this evening?" Everyone accepted, delicious food and numerous bottles of wine appeared and it was a challenge to finally get our guests to leave. (Although the pink bathroom remains, the rest of the suite has now been totally refurbished; you can overnight there for a mere £7,150.)

Later, my parents met David's children, Simon, 6, and Bridget, 5, for the first time. Leaning down to Bridget, my mother said: "And you can call me Big Mary Moore". With a spirit of independence that became part of her trademark, Bridget replied regally: "We already have one Mary Moore in the family. You shall be called Sally." And, to my father, Robert, "And you shall be called Bobbie" – the family names they retained thereafter.

We were often joined by David's interesting but somewhat formidable mother, Frances, widow of an Anglican vicar called Reginald. Meeting my parents for the first time – just off the plane from America – she stated she was rather fond of Americans. In fact, it would seem, rather too fond. She went on to describe a rip-roaring World War II affair she had enjoyed with an American

Frances Redfern (left), her sister, Mary, and my mother in between

Army officer while still married to the vicar. Apparently when she and her lover confronted Reginald in his office with the news of their affair, he looked up from his desk and said: "This is really momentous news. Please fall to your knees and join me in prayer." They were then shooed out of his office so he could continue composing his Sunday sermon. Mercifully, I discovered that my parents, both suffering from jet lag, had snoozed their way though this part of the family gathering.

Later, Frances left the vicar for a scientologist and when we first met she was best friends with a chap who was a dedicated Druid. This came in handy when I was asked by Pan Am to guide a group of American spiritualists, led by their invisible Native American spiritual guide, to relevant sites around London. They particularly wanted to visit Primrose Hill as it was, they said, situated on a mystical ley line and it was the Spring Equinox. And there was Frances' friend, John, dressed in a long white robe, dancing in a circle with other Druids. The Americans all professed to be most impressed by my local connections. However, I heard not a word from their invisible spiritual guide.

And then there were the extended family events. One of the Redfern cousins married a young Russian "princess" in a unique ceremony presided over by two clergymen, the Russian Orthodox priest's marital message accompanied by much chanting and clouds of incense and the Anglican, possibly mindful of the father of the groom being head of his local hunt meet, going on about leading a horse to water which somehow seemed inappropriate.

Then we progressed to a grand reception where a group of mysterious-looking Russians, one of them an actor who portrayed villains in various James Bond films, huddled conspiratorially in the corner while David's flamboyant Auntie Mary, adorned in a feather boa, flirted her way around the room. David's bearded elder brother Paul arrived belatedly and inexplicably in a kilt and cousin Peter, a dwarf, appeared to be enjoying his unique vantage point surrounded by numerous young ladies in mini-skirts.

On another occasion, Frances, David, the children and I were asked to accompany her brother-in-law, John, to the unveiling of a plaque to her late husband in one of the Yorkshire churches he had served as vicar. John's presence was particularly welcome as, following a distinguished career as a foreign correspondent for the *Daily Express*, he had been the newspaper's religious correspondent until, according to family tittle-tattle, he had disgraced himself by going on a bender in Jerusalem while researching a story called "In the footsteps of the Pope".

Obviously unaware of this misadventure, the rather dour parishioners asked us to join them in the church hall, where John was asked to describe his most moving religious moment. Pondering briefly, he said it was attending holy communion in New York's Greenwich Village. No standard old wafers and wine there, said John; the priest had announced a choice of cocktails and canapés and then everyone was issued with funny hats, confetti and noise makers. "And that," said John, "is what Christianity is all about." To a resounding silence, Frances saved the day by announcing "Well, we really must rush to catch the train back to London," and we hustled out the door.

I was able a few years later to catch up with John in his West Country home base of Cerne Abbas, best known for the image of a naked giant equipped with a huge penis carved in chalk on a nearby hillside. As we sat drinking gin in his local pub he stated that the community was too conventional for his taste – the local authorities had rejected his proposal that an equivalent female image be carved on a nearby hill.

What would it have been? I asked, and he explained: a Hollywood film-inspired Marilyn Monroe standing over the air grate, her skirts flying up above her thighs. And if a chalk carving proved environmentally unpopular, the image could be accomplished by planting daffodil bulbs. "Then every spring she could bloom into life," he announced to all those in the pub who greeted the suggestion with stony silence.

Frances arrived for our first family Christmas lunch bearing, with great reverence, a large homemade Christmas pudding which, she announced, I must steam for a precise period of time. Otherwise it would be ruined. Then the doorbell rang, revealing two forlorn-looking young men who presented me with a scribbled note explaining they were deaf mutes en route to a party, but, alas, their car had broken down in front of our house.

Summoning them into the front hall and scribbling a note back, I suggested that a call to their automobile breakdown service would be logical, but after numerous rings received no reply. Then I scribbled another suggestion: why didn't I phone their friends hosting the party and ask for someone to come and collect them? The response was negative: all their fellow party goers were also deaf mutes. So ushering them into the living room I gestured for them to sit down with the family while I phoned the police. As they rapidly signed to one another Simon and Bridget, thinking it was a game, started "signing" too while Frances, looking quite cross, began to tap her watch.

The doorbell rang again and this time it was two young uniformed police officers who joined the seated group. When I suggested they take my fellow guests to their party, they said they were not allowed to do this. Desperate for a solution, I summoned the two deaf mutes into the hall, wrote them a note explaining that the police had kindly offered to take them to the party if they would quickly get into the back of the police car. Then I returned to the police in mock dismay to explain that, as I was unable to communicate with my other guests, they were waiting for them in the car. Meanwhile the Christmas pudding was ruined and Frances remained silent during much of the meal.

On another occasion when the doorbell rang I found a small Indian man standing on the threshold waving an admonishing finger at me. "So who's been a silly person then?" he asked. It turned out that David was totally unaware that he had dropped his wallet in the street while we were out shopping the hour before.

Inviting our benefactor in and offering a monetary award, which he refused, I suggested he join the children, David and me for tea, which actually consisted of an early dinner of cauliflower cheese and mashed potatoes. "I have never been in an English home before," said our guest, in wonder. "And how interesting to see what the English eat ... goodness, gracious me!"

But all was not fun and games on Holland Park Avenue. Early on the morning of October 23, 1975, we woke to the sound of an explosion so massive that it shattered the window in the front room of our flat. Soon the police cordoned off the street and journalists began knocking on our door to ask if they could use our flat as a vantage point. It transpired that the IRA had placed a bomb under the car of Sir Hugh Fraser, the prominent Conservative politician, who lived in nearby Campden Hill Square. It was set off when a dog being walked by another neighbor, noted cancer researcher Gorden Hamilton Fairley, sniffed under the car. Both were killed. If it had happened moments later when Sir Hugh was due to leave for work accompanied by his house guest, Caroline Kennedy, both would have perished.

David and I frequently traveled together or separately as he covered jazz festivals throughout the UK, France and the USA and I continued to go on PR assignments for Pan Am and write regularly for American magazines and British newspapers, covering places as far afield as Japan, Kenya and Thailand. And as David's business expanded, we spent an increasing amount of time in Manhattan, where I became quite fascinated by the professional backgrounds of the local taxi drivers who, unlike their London counterparts, often seemed to have no idea of local geography.

Hailing a cab from Midtown Manhattan to Newark Airport just across the Hudson River, I was told by the driver he had no idea how to get there so I had to direct him through the Holland Tunnel. En route, he revealed, not surprisingly, that he really wasn't a professional cab driver at all; he was a medical student who had delivered a baby only the night before on the very seat in which I was ensconced.

Another driver, who had difficulties navigating me to a friend's house in Brooklyn, revealed that he was really an Afghan importer of garden furniture, and on another occasion a lady cab driver, whose taxi light was turned off, took pity on me standing alone and forlornly waving in the rain. Dressed in an apron with flour on her hands, she announced she was a Jewish mother who was just rushing off to get some basic ingredients so she could prepare dinner for "my son, the dentist". Not only did she get me to the right address – and on time – but she also gave me the recipe for her special borscht.

But my most-memorable experience was with a jolly cabbie who picked me up one day in Midtown. Discovering that I lived in London and was relatively new in the Big Apple, he asked if I was in a big rush. If not, he would like to take me on a free drive by his favorite places in Manhattan. As I thanked him and settled back in my seat, he offered me a choice of an Old Fashioned, a Bloody Mary or a Gin and Tonic. "Sometimes I get really bored," he explained. "So I keep a cooler in the front seat and when I pick up someone I think might be interesting to talk to I just offer them a drink to make their ride even more interesting." And after two large Bloody Marys, it certainly was.

One summer weekend, David, who was a devotee of the UK's public footpath system and of camping out in general, suggested that we go camping somewhere in New England. So we found a camping shop in Greenwich Village and purchased the basics: two sleeping bags, a tent pole, some mosquito netting to hang from it and a couple of water bottles. Our destination, he decided would be Mount Greylock, the tallest mountain in Massachusetts. Deep in a woodland we found a delightful area that had a flat place for us to place our sleeping bags, a campfire area and a nearby stream. As nobody was around, David suggested we go skinny dipping, so, abandoning our clothes, we were happily splashing away at about hip level when we suddenly heard the marching and singing sound of a happy troop of Boy Scouts, who stood giggling and pointing at us for some time before their disapproving Scout masters moved them on. "Damn it," said David. "One of those little buggers stole my Swiss Army Knife!"

We then moved on in search of a state park camping site David had found on a Massachusetts map. Driving slowly at twilight in search of a rural road turn-off, we suddenly heard a siren, saw flashing lights and found ourselves accosted by a traffic cop, hands on his holsters. "You were driving in a suspicious matter," he announced in a menacing manner.

After David explained, in his British accent, that we were benign tourists merely seeking a camp site for the night our now-friendly policeman insisted on guiding us through the woods to the cabin of a forest warden. Emerging in red flannel pyjamas and rather grumpily getting into his truck, he and the cop led us in convoy into a moonlit glade, their vehicle sirens slicing through the otherwise silent night.

There we were greeted by alarmed looking campers who had emerged from their elegant camper vans and tents to view our arrival. David and I then furtively disappeared into the surrounding woodland to change into our night clothes – I emerged in a black negligee and David in boxer shorts, scratching and complaining that the log he had rested on was apparently full of biting insects known as chiggers. (I later discovered to my dismay that I apparently had rubbed up against some poison ivy.)

Our fellow campers were obviously not impressed when we put up a pole from which we fanned out mosquito netting, having rejected buying a tent as a waste of money for only one camping weekend. Later in the trip, we went to a drive-in movie and somehow got the tent pole stuck into the car's indented horn, much to the dismay of our fellow filmgoers. Perhaps we were not well-suited for rural or small-town life.

Nor were our travel misadventures limited to the USA. On our Brazilian honeymoon at Rio's Copacabana Beach, I returned to the hotel for a nap, leaving David sunbathing on a beach towel.

Suddenly he spotted a bikini-clad beauty strolling through the surf and, certain she would make an ideal record-cover photo, grabbed his camera, leapt up, asked the Brazilian sitting on an adjacent beach towel to "please watch after my things" and sped down the strand.

When he returned, his things, including a considerable amount of money and the passport he had inexplicably taken to the beach, had disappeared. "I asked you to watch after my things," he lamented to the man on the adjoining beach towel. "*Si, señor,*" was the answer, "I watched as the little boys came out of the favela and took your things."

At my insistence, we traveled to the Copacabana police station where we were courteously greeting by a police chief straight out of a vintage Hollywood film. Elegantly dressed in a spotless navy-blue uniform adorned with gold epaulettes, he entertained us in impressive English with gruesome stories of local murders while decapitating his cigar in one of those special little machines. His job, he explained, was to keep the local crime statistics as low as possible, so if we were reasonable people and simply filled out the form stating that the valuables were lost, he would have no problem signing the necessary papers enabling David to quickly replace his passport and claim insurance for the missing money. If, on the other hand, theft was mentioned on the form, it might take a very, very long time indeed for our new friend to sort out our problem. You can probably guess what decision we made.

Over the forthcoming years it became obvious that not all was well at Pan Am, for, although it was the world's largest airline and the unofficial flag carrier for the USA, fuel and other expenses were high and, after international airline deregulation in 1978, it also faced stiff competition from other American airlines. Unlike Pan Am, they had extensive domestic networks that could feed into their new international flights.

While searching for a domestic partner, Pan Am began to cut back its routes, equipment and staff, and eventually it became time for me to go. (In 1991, following an unsuccessful merger with National Airlines and the 1988 fatal terrorist bomb explosion of Pan Am Flight 103 over Lockerbie, Scotland, the 64-year-old airline stopped flying.)

Rio de Janeiro's Copacabana Beach, site of our
eventful Brazilian honeymoon
(Photo: Catarina Belova/Shutterstock)

New Airline Adventures and the Birth of Mark

As one airline flew out of my life, another flew in. A former Pan Am colleague asked if I would help his brother promote East African Airways, which was flying from London to Nairobi and onwards to destinations in Kenya, Uganda and Tanzania. Although relatively little-known in the UK, EAA had the distinction of being the first non-UK based airline to fly a member of the British Royal Family – the new Queen Elizabeth II – on her way back to London after the death of her father, King George VI, in 1952.

I flew first to Nairobi to meet the airline's in-house PR man; then I began to explore the country, looking for story ideas ... and there were so many: lively Nairobi, exotic Mombasa, the seductive coastal resorts, the great national parks that were filled with magnificent animals, and the wealth of quite different native groups, from the Kikuyu to the Masai. Sometimes I traveled with Anne, a new, Kenya-based friend who was a location finder for Hollywood films.

Over one memorable weekend in 1975 we watched Sidney Poitier and Michael Caine film a night-time escape scene in *The Wilby Conspiracy* and then joined them and their charming wives for dinner in the Mount Kenya Club. On another occasion, Anne and I spent a fascinating time in a Masai village located on the estate of her wealthy Belgian boyfriend.

And then there were the times I was asked by an African game warden to go to a drug store and collect a laxative for a constipated tiger cub and – when on a press trip to an elephant reserve – I found myself consoling a young urban-based Kenyan journalist who couldn't provide the herd of cattle demanded as "bride money" by his prospective father-in-law.

A challenge arose when David was commissioned by the airline to take photos of glamorous British models embarking from an aircraft in Mombasa. He and I arrived first, enjoyed a few idyllic days at the coastal Diani Beach Resort, and when the day came for the three British models and David's assistant to arrive via Nairobi, another journalist and I hitched a ride with a bush pilot up the coast to the exotic island of Lamu. Just as we were settling in to research our respective travel stories, another bush pilot arrived with an obviously rapidly-scribbled note from David: "Come back immediately … in terrible trouble."

It transpired that David had awoken in the middle of the night in a remote beach villa to discover himself surrounded by several semi-naked men armed with machetes who were taking his passport, money and valuable Hasselblad cameras. There was no way to summon help until the next morning as the car ferry linking the site over an inlet with the main resort areas didn't run at night. Meanwhile, his models and assistant had apparently missed the connecting flight to Mombasa and he didn't know where they were.

I found myself in Nairobi tracking down the rest of the group and trying to find someone to loan me a Hasselblad. Luckily, while researching a series of articles on women photographers around the world, I had made friends with a local wildlife photographer who directed me to another photographer who also shot with Hasselblads. Over dinner, he agreed to lend me his cameras, which I then got insured and sent, along with the models and assistant, to Mombasa.

Once back in London, things became much calmer and on March 2, 1976, dear Mark was born and life changed in a new and even more fulfilling way. I began writing about traveling with children, including Simon, now 11, and Bridget, 10, not only within Britain but also in such places as France, Norway and, later, the USA. And I was offered a job as a PR executive for the London branch of the USTS (the United States Travel Service) by the major media promotion agency, Carl Byoir.

Partly because of my airline PR experience, we then picked up the PR account for Braniff, the flamboyant Texas-based airline scheduled to launch its "Big Orange" Boeing 747s from Dallas-Fort Worth into London in early 1978. Fronted by handsome, silver-haired chairman Harding Lawrence, who looked like he could have stepped out of the cast of *Dallas* or *Dynasty*, Braniff was on a roll to revolutionize air travel.

Forget the subdued colors of other airlines' aircraft, its 747s and other aircraft would be vividly painted, sometimes based on designs by famous artist Alexander Calder; its First Class seats would be leather; and its cabin crew would be initially clothed in flamboyant Space Age-inspired Emilio Pucci and later in chic Halston ultra-suede. Offering highly competitive fares, the airline also planned to rapidly expand its routes to Europe, Latin America and elsewhere.

However, there was a controversy as to where its Dallas/Fort Worth flights should land in London. Braniff insisted on Heathrow, whereas the British government demanded it be Gatwick. This inspired an *Evening Standard* cartoon showing a cowboy representing Braniff, hands on his holsters, confronting a British bureaucrat representing the Civil Aviation Authority. The caption read: "Look, old boy. I don't know how you negotiate in Texas --- but!" Finally, after what the Texans call a "Mexican Standoff", Braniff backed down and agreed on Gatwick, with the VIP pre-inaugural flight scheduled for February 29, 1978.

Realizing that the airline's strong Texas image made it distinctive, Braniff's PR team on both sides of the Atlantic decided to make the London arrival of its "Big Orange" 747 as memorable and colorful as possible. The Windsor Barracks Regional Band was hired to welcome the passengers, who included the mayors of Dallas and Fort Worth, with a rousing rendition of *The Yellow Rose of Texas*. And as they disembarked down the steps, all the VIPs on board wore gigantic Stetsons, which I had rented and delivered to the plane in advance. It resulted in front page newspaper and prime-time TV coverage in the UK and elsewhere.

BRANIFF INTERNATIONAL

August 7, 1979

Mrs. Mary Redfern
Carl Byoir & Associates, Ltd.
Berkeley Square House
Berkeley Square
London, W1X 6EQ
England

Dear Mary,

This letter is intended in a small way to express my personal appreciation as well as that of the company for your inspired efforts in successfully launching Braniff in the U K. and on the Continent.

You are a true public relations and journalistic professional with the unique capability of being able to create as well as to develop and execute. I have been particularly impressed with your dealings with the important journalists and their appreciation of your news sense.

Most importantly, you did exactly the job we asked you to do in establishing Braniff in the European marketplace in a short time.

I hope our paths cross many times in the future and perhaps events will bring about future associations If at any time I could commend your public relations and publicity abilities to others I would be pleased and honored to do so.

Best wishes and kindest regards

Sincerely,

JLC/m

Jere L. Cox
Vice President, Public Relations

World Headquarters
Braniff Boulevard
Dallas-Fort Worth Airport
Texas 75261 U.S.A.

A letter of commendation from Braniff

Numerous press trips followed, not only to Dallas and Fort Worth but also to other colorful cities such as San Antonio, with its historic River Walk; music-rich Austin; Bandera, surrounded by dude ranches; the northern Panhandle, where we viewed the musical *Texas* set deep in the Palo Duro Canyon; Laredo, with trips across the Rio Grande to Mexico; and even float trips down the river from the tiny town of Lajitas, tucked away in the Big Bend country in the south-western corner of the state.

Enjoying time with David and baby Mark

Mark, age 4, on the road with mum and dad

Upon arrival there, the group of journalists I accompanied were encouraged to offer a beer to the mayor, who turned out to be a rather truculent goat, before putting on our bathing suits, boarding our float boat and heading down the Rio Grande. The river turned out to be not so grand and, except for a few rapids, rather boringly calm. So, reinforced by a few beers and inspired by stories of the Mexican "wetbacks" who illegally swam into America, we decided to leap off the boat and swim into Mexico, carrying with us some beach towels in a waterproof bag.

No sooner did we hit shore in what appeared to be a totally uninhabited area than we heard shouts of "gringos, gringos" echoing through the nearby scrubland and canyons. Then a group of small Mexicans in huge sombreros magically appeared with a donkey, which I was invited to hop on, swathed in a towel. Escorted along dirt paths to a remote village, we found the residents snoozing in their afternoon siesta, but suddenly everyone sprang into action. A small mariachi band and bottles of beer materialized, spicy sausages were loaded onto a grill and we held a bilingual sing-along. Thereafter all my journalists were sworn to secrecy – after all, what we had done was quite illegal ... but great fun!

Riding herd on British travel writers in Texas

Then there was the time when we included two university students from Aberdeen, Scotland, in a press trip to Dallas and Fort Worth. They had entered a UK-wide university fund-raising competition to see who could travel the farthest distance for free so we thought it would be good PR if that destination was Texas. However, when they arrived in kilts at the airport I discovered to my alarm that both were punks with alarming green spiked hair and razor blades dangling from their ears.

They turned out to be really nice young lads but that didn't protect them from being insulted by pool-playing cowboys when we entered a funky Fort Worth Cowtown bar. "Oh, look at the ladies in their skirts and green hair," jeered the cowboys, waving their pool cues provocatively in the air. With his Scottish masculinity insulted, one of the Aberdeen lads punched a cowboy in the jaw and all hell broke loose. I had to intervene and the punks and cowboys ended up great friends, spending the night out on the town which, alas, made the young Scots slightly the worse for wear when they arrived the next morning to present tartan scarves and bottles of Scotch to the mayors of Dallas and Fort Worth.

As Braniff expanded its routes to France, Belgium, Holland and Germany I was sent off to establish PR links in those countries, and then, in 1979, the airline pulled off a real coup, partnering with both British Airways and Air France to take over their respective Concordes at Washington-Dulles International Airport and fly them on subsonically to Dallas-Fort Worth.

I was on board with a group of British journalists and what a thrill it was to land on the DFW runway with an Air France Concorde touching down beside us on a parallel runway. And what a challenge it was, in my fractured French, to explain the Texas lifestyle to the French journalists who then joined us. That was particularly the case when we arrived at a Dallas restaurant to be met by a gum-chewing cowgirl receptionist who, until I intervened, attempted to cut off the Frenchmen's designer ties with a pair of shears. It was the custom, she explained, to add them to the displays nailed to the wall.

Eventually, both Braniff and I began to run out of steam; Braniff, because it had overextended itself both financially and geographically – in one day alone it launched 32 new routes to 16 new cities – and in my case, because in spite of having consistently good child care, I wanted to spend more time with lively young Mark. Also, David needed some back-up help while expanding his business to include a commercial picture library and processing studios for both black and white and color pictures.

The Launch of a Unique Travel Magazine

An early edition of Holiday USA & Canada

Luckily, I had been approached by two publisher brothers, Derek and Peter Shephard, who, although they had never been to North America, decided it was time to add a travel magazine about the USA and Canada to their portfolio. The first such publication in the UK, it was to be called *Holiday USA & Canada* and I would be the launch and ongoing editor. Although I chose to remain freelance, I was soon regularly traveling to their office in London's Highgate, where, frequently reinforced by glasses of champagne poured by Derek, I worked side by side with the editors of *Majesty*, crammed with features about European royalty, a glossy British travel magazine and crossword journals.

I had also been asked by yet another former Pan Am colleague to help him promote Air Florida's new service from London to Miami and, later, Jamaica and Haiti.

One of the press trips I organized and accompanied was particularly memorable. Scheduled to include a visit to the Kennedy Space Center, where we would witness a manned rocket launch, it unfortunately coincided with a hurricane. This not only canceled the space launch but trapped us in the Florida Keys, where our hotel complex was flooded, forcing several rival journalists to unhappily share beds in the unaffected bungalows.

Then, after we moved to the elegant Cheeca Lodge on Islamorada, one of the tabloid journalists marched into my room in the early evening, waving a bottle of tequila and announcing he had "not been able to sleep alone" since his traumatic stint in Vietnam (I later discovered he had only been there two days). Nudging me amorously onto the balcony he then noticed to his horror that the underwear he had been drying on the neighboring balcony had been carried by a breeze into the nearby palm trees. He was not impressed when I suggested he immediately rush to the hotel's fishing shop, secure a fishing pole and hook up his undies … and the next day he flew back to London in a huff, announcing that his presence was urgently required on Fleet Street.

Meanwhile, David was working on his first book of photographs and frequently visiting Germany "on business". When it was published in 1980, it included a tribute to someone called Caroline, without whom, it said, David could not have produced this book. It later turned out she was his Germany-based British girlfriend. Things came to a head when my old friend Morag, now married to a British journalist and living in New York, flew with unwelcome news to Virginia, where Mark and I were on holiday.

When having drinks with David in Manhattan, he had revealed to her that he was aware that I was unhappy but that didn't matter. I could move back to America and he would take Mark to live with him and his girlfriend. Both alarmed and irate, I returned to London, packed all his possessions in a trunk, sent it to his office, changed the locks on the door and sued for divorce, citing Caroline as his co-respondent.

In fact, our marriage had been disintegrating for quite some time. What had appeared initially to be the ideal partnership of a writer and photographer who loved each other, America, exploring Britain's public footpaths and travel in general, proved not to be a real partnership. Other than the three children whom we both loved, it transpired that we intellectually and spiritually had little in common and were increasingly moving in different directions.

Mark and I moved into the first home I ever owned, an attractive maisonette in Notting Hill; Mark continued at the elementary school he loved and I continued to work as both a writer and publicist. Then, once again, everything began to change.

My father died suddenly from a heart attack, and Air Florida, already struggling financially, was literally dealt its own death blow when on January 13, 1982, one of its domestic flights, taking off during a snowstorm from Washington DC's National Airport, crashed into the icy Potomac River leaving only five survivors. (In 1984, the airline ceased trading.)

Meanwhile, a dual-nationality couple of publishers I wrote for pointed out that as Mark was born overseas, the son of an American mother and a foreign father, he would not legally obtain American citizenship unless we spent some time back in America (that law has long since changed). And, as my divorce was finalized in July 1983 and I had received the Shephards' blessing to edit *Holiday USA & Canada* from America, I headed once again back to Virginia.

Back to the Future on a Virginia Farm

You will have already read about our arrival back in Virginia. So how did we settle in? I reinforced my decision for the move back to my home state by tongue-in-cheek reading the anonymous but famous Virginia mantra hanging on the farmhouse's parlor wall: "To be a Virginian by birth, marriage, adoption, or even on one's mother's side, is an introduction to any State in the Union, a passport to any Foreign Country and a benediction from Above." Then I took stock of the situation.

On the positive side, we were living with my very-welcoming, amusing if sometimes-sparky mother in a beautiful old house that had 11 well-decorated and furnished rooms, a modern kitchen and lovely views from back and front porches over rolling farmland and Jump Mountain, rising on our land and named, according to local lore, for a Native American maiden, who, seeing her lover die in battle below, leapt to her death from its summit.

This was remarkably different from my weekend and holiday time spent at the farm when I was a child living in Roanoke. Then, we cooked on open log fires, ate by candlelight, read by kerosene lamps, pumped water for drinking, cooking and bathing from the cistern on the back patio and, when nature called, trotted down a dirt path to the outside "johnny house". That was because the old bachelor uncle who had last resided at Walkerlands with two family retainers living in the attic had never installed plumbing or electricity. So, when they inherited it, mother and dad had to completely modernize the house while overseeing the demolition of most of the derelict surrounding farm buildings, including, to my mother's dismay, a grand old barn, retaining only the side yard log kitchen of the original house.

Upon retirement mother set up a local readers' club, wrote book reviews for the Lexington weekly newspaper and occasionally turned her hand to short-story writing, which included a quite creepy yarn entitled *Doris, the Baby Vampire*. Meanwhile, dad continued with home improvements, became an elder in the nearby Presbyterian church and helped various Virginia family members with legal matters.

But then there was the challenging question of how Mark would settle in. Would he find new friends? Where would he go to school? And what would I do for intellectual stimulation when not writing, commissioning and editing copy for *Holiday USA & Canada*?

Luckily, on previous visits we had become friends with the out-of-state families who had bought Stoneyfoot, a large tract of land in the forest at the end of the dead-end road that bisected our land. Living first communally in an old rundown farmhouse – while the local farmers referred to them as "them there hippies" – and then building their individual wooden homes, our neighbors soon absorbed us into their lives.

There were hikes up a nearby mountain to visit our local "hermit" (actually a well-educated, semi-retired preacher whose rustic, self-built house was well stocked with treats for the children), picnics by the Maury River that flowed through a deep mountain pass, and horseback riding lessons for Mark. When autumn came, Mark could join the other children on the yellow school bus which picked them up at the end of the lane and took them via a connecting bus to the village of Fairfield, site of the Rockbridge County elementary school.

There was just one problem: Mark wouldn't get on the bus. As he adamantly continued his resistance, I drove him to and from school until one day Stoneyfoot neighbor Lee Merrill, father of two, said firmly to Mark: "Young man, you are causing your mother a lot of grief, so on you go," and he hoisted Mark, in floods of tears, on to the bus. About a half-hour later the lady bus driver, Mrs Moneymaker, phoned. "Hello Miz Redfern. You don't need to worry about that kid. He got to school and he's gonna be alright."

Meanwhile, I persuaded the head of the journalism school at Lexington's then all-male Washington and Lee University to let me audit a TV production course, and I was invited to a meeting in an historic Lexington inn by Martha Doss, the local tourism director. At the meeting were innkeepers from up and down the Shenandoah Valley discussing how they could attract more visitors to their picturesque but often-quite-remote hostelries. "Why don't you form a group and call it *The Inns of the Shenandoah Valley*," I suggested. "Then you could jointly promote the idea of spending time in one or more inns in this famous valley."

I visited all the inns, which included a farmhouse-based establishment offering horseback trekking into the Blue Ridge Mountains; a charming converted gristmill tucked away in a tiny village; an atmospheric former tavern; and a modern mountaintop chalet adjacent to a ski resort. One of my Stoneyfoot neighbors,

Main Street, Lexington, Virginia
(Photo: Chris Weisler)

Lee's wife Jane, an art teacher, then made delightful sketches of each inn and we produced a quite fetching fold-out brochure to distribute to all the Virginia state visitor centers along the valley's main Interstate 81 and at various travel trade shows.

Later, having written an article on *Bed and Breakfasts with Uncle Sam* for the London *Times*, I was asked to speak at a conference on how American B&Bs could attract foreign visitors. This inspired a London colleague and me to set up a pioneering but short-lived accommodation service we called Host Home North America, sort of an early Airbnb.

THE NEW YORK DAILY NEWS, JUNE 2, 1985

Overnighting in Virginia inns

If you're planning a visit to Virginia's Shenandoah Valley, consider staying in one of the area's historic inns, 12 of which have banded together to form an association. Some of the inns are located near major highways, others are tucked away in remote valleys.

All are unique. A case in point is the Belle Grae Inn in Staunton, a huge Victorian mansion

THE WASHINGTON POST
MAY 13, 1984

Fearless Traveler

Shenandoah Inns, India, Camping, Skiing, D-Day and Assorted Tours

By James T. Yenckel

The attractions of rural Virginia should become more accessible to local travelers with the recent formation of an informal organization called Inns of the Shenandoah Valley. Twelve independent inns, stretching from Middletown at the valley's northern end to Lexington in the south, have banded together to promote their establishments and the historic, scenic and recreational qualities of the valley and bordering mountains.

Such lodging associations have become something of a trend in the inn business as a way to compete with much larger hotel and motel chains. Most of the Shenandoah inns can accommodate fewer than two dozen guests. Their first cooperative effort, in which they share costs, is an information brochure about the inns and the valley, due out by mid-June.

What it means for reservation seekers is that first

THE CHRISTIAN SCIENCE MONITOR.
March 24, 1986

Two inns added to historic group

Virginia's Inns of the Shenandoah Valley recently observed its second anniversary by adding two new members, bringing to 12 the number of inns pledged to provide and promote fine lodging throughout the valley.

The new members help reflect the history and ambiance for which the association was already known. Woodstock's Inn at Narrow Passage, originally a pioneer's log home, later served as headquarters for Civil War Gen. Stonewall Jackson and as a girl's school. The multigabled Vine Cottage Inn in Hot Springs was built around 1900, only a 10-minutes walk from the renow

New Friends and Family Connections

As I got to know more of my neighbors, I began to be invited to more local events. One beautiful autumn afternoon, Baltimore-based writer and editor Mame Warren, one of the part-time Stoneyfoot residents, married her beau, Henry Harris, in the forest. As they stood on a small stone bridge spanning what they called "The Stream of Consciousness", the ceremony was performed by architect Lee, inexplicably garbed in a mandarin robe and crowned by a straw hat topped by a pineapple (a symbol of hospitality in the American South). The wedding march, played by a bluegrass band, was the Beatles' "Will you still need me, will you still feed me when I'm 64?" And then we all adjourned to the communal barn for a fantastic meal of soul food prepared by some African-American cooks from Lexington.

When February arrived, another neighbor, David Beebe, and I tapped Walkerlands' grove of sugar maple trees. The thin sap was boiled for hours into a sweet, heavy syrup, freshly-ground buckwheat flour was obtained from historic nearby Wade's Mill and the neighbors and their children were summoned to a pancake party followed by sledding down the slopes behind the farmhouse.

On the long summer evenings, mother and I would lie in neighboring hammocks on the front porch listening to the sounds of the cicadas, crickets and creek frogs as she told me stories of her childhood summers there years ago. Life on the farm, she said, had been orchestrated by her favorite aunt, Maggie, who roared around the neighborhood in a Model T Ford, tending to everyone's business until she ran over a pig and, humiliated, went back to driving a horse and carriage. A spinster, she had been deeply in love with a Presbyterian missionary who married another woman, who died of fever when he took her to Africa. "I would have never let him down by dying," Aunt Maggie used to tell mother.

Grandmother Fannie Moore Walker (far right, second row),
her Walkerlands' parents and siblings

And then there was her dapper, mischievous brother, Uncle Tommy, who remained a confirmed bachelor as the great love of his life had also married another, as well as other aunts and uncles and the live-in African-American housekeeper and cook Cornelia, whose lively little daughter, Charlotte, became mother's best friend. In fact, said mother, she refused to go to the birthday party Aunt Maggie had organized for her as Charlotte had not been invited.

When Charlotte reached marital age, Aunt Maggie and many of her match-making friends were concerned as there were few young African-American men in the community. Finally, good-natured but mentally-challenged Robert Alexander materialized and his marriage to Charlotte was held in the community's chapel in nearby Brownsburg. One of mother's cousins, Jen Wade, the stepmother of the previously mentioned Steve Heffelfinger, played the organ and when Charlotte walked down the aisle, she was accompanied by Cornelia, proudly bearing aloft the framed marriage certificate.

The circuit-riding pastor said: "Will you Robert take Cornelia Harris as your wedded wife?" and when Charlotte kept protesting "I'm Charlotte, I'm Charlotte," she was shushed, the protest was ignored several times more and thus Robert married "Cornelia". When they went outside and, as the wedding photo was made and the flash gun went off, Robert threw up his white-gloved hands in horror and shouted, "Oh Lord, Oh Lord, I've been shot!"

In spite of their quite different personalities and intellects Charlotte and Robert lived in relative harmony in Staunton just up the Shenandoah Valley and she and mother kept in touch regularly. One day, mother, by then in her mid-70s, announced: "Little black Charlotte is coming for a visit." And a dignified, considerably older Charlotte arrived in a fetching grey wig and a fox fur wrap – although it was mid-summer – accompanied by her handsome young nephew.

Seated in adjacent rocking chairs, she and my mother began telling stories of their childhood. "Do you remember when we used to go to that place down by the river where the white folks stayed in the summer," giggled Charlotte. "I used to get up and dance and folks would say 'Look at that little black girl dance; she sure can dance!' and they would give me nickels. And then you would get up and dance and they would say, 'That little white girl really can't dance for nothing. Do we have to give her nickels too?'" And mother would laugh too, although not quite as enthusiastically as Charlotte.

While dad was still alive, we had made a visit with mother to Charlotte's and Robert's house in Staunton. Concerned that their house was not warm enough in the winter, dad had given them a new furnace, so when we arrived on a hot summer day Robert turned it up full blast to show us how effective it was. As we sat sweating profusely in their living room, a large African-American man in jeans and a baseball hat suddenly appeared at the back door, looked at us and shouted, "Who are all these honkies, Charlotte?"

Obviously embarrassed, she introduced us; he sat down next to me and said: "Give me five, sister" and after we slapped extended palms together we briefly discussed the weather and he departed. As we drove back to Walkerlands, I said to my mother: "What did you think of Charlotte's boyfriend?" to which she indignantly replied: "Don't be ridiculous – Charlotte was brought up a good Presbyterian; she would never be unfaithful to Robert!" But a year or so later when Charlotte was briefly in the hospital and I paid her a visit, the guy in the baseball hat turned up, too, pretending at the admission desk to be her husband. *C'est la vie*, I thought and, with a twinge of conscience, accompanied him to her bedside.

Later, when I asked mother what had happened to all of the siblings of Great Aunt Maggie, her brother, Tom, and my grandmother, Fannie Moore, she explained that most of them moved west to places as far afield as Texas, the Midwest and California. However, many of their descendants or even more distant relatives occasionally dropped by the "old home place" to meet my mother and have their photos taken in the Jacobean-style John Walker chair, reputedly brought to America from Scotland by the first Walker immigrant in 1728.

And indeed, during my time at Walkerlands, a family of Illinois Walkers dropped by, as did a young Walker from Hawaii with his Japanese wife, who, hands folded and bowing to my mother, said in a sing-song voice: "Bet you never think you have Japanese cousin!" But perhaps the most memorable visit was from two immensely-fat old ladies and a young man who arrived unannounced from somewhere in the Midwest, claiming to be our distant cousins.

As mother was napping and I was on the phone, Mark, knowing that Virginians were always expected to be hospitable, presented the guests with the only refreshments he could find, glasses of lemonade and animal crackers, served on a silver tray. In return, he was let into the confidence of one of the ladies' son, who revealed that he had been visited by aliens while living in a trailer in the Arizona desert.

On another memorable day, a man named Bil Gilbert arrived to announce he was researching a book about Joseph Walker, grandson of the emigrant John Walker who had settled at Walkerlands. Mother pulled out the old farmhouse diaries to see what they would reveal about the early Walkers and, meanwhile, Bil told us what he knew: Joe, who was born in Tennessee, became the sheriff of Independence, Missouri. He was also a renowned explorer, a developer of the famous westward Santa Fe Trail, and the first non-Native American to see and camp in the Yosemite Valley, site of one of today's most spectacular US national parks.

Along the way, he partnered with a Native American woman and then, with his brother, Joel, and his family, became one of the first Americans to settle in California, then part of Mexico. The resulting book, *Westering Man – The Life of Joseph Walker,* was published in 1983; later, I was sent a picture of Joe from the PR for Yosemite National Park and came upon a rather dashing portrait of him in the Joslyn Art Museum in Omaha, Nebraska.

Then there were our local cousins, three generations of the McLaughlin family who ran a children's camp each summer on the adjacent farm known as Maxwelton. Among its offerings were horseback riding, swimming, boating, mountain climbing, archery, tennis and arts and crafts, which, as a teenager, I taught one summer. The McLaughlin matriarch was charming Rosa, reputedly descended from the Indian "princess" Pocahontas, and the mother of five children. Surrounded by boisterous grandchildren, family dogs and swarms of young campers, she remained the calm, warm, perfect hostess, sometimes inviting us to join family meals on the big house's screened-in back porch or to swim in the hilltop lake, surrounded by the campers' cabins.

Mountain man and explorer Joseph Walker
(Photo: Yosemite National Park)

JOSEPH REDDEFORD WALKER

We also had a unique family heritage in common with the McLaughlins: we are all descended from the original Mary Moore, who at age nine – the only survivor of a family massacre many miles away in south-west Virginia – was kidnapped by the Shawnee Indians, sold as a slave across the border into Canada, rescued by a family friend and brought back to this area of Virginia, where she founded a dynasty that included many a namesake Mary Moore, a fact that led to some confusion at the rare extended family reunions.

Many years later, I headed with my son, his wife, Wendy, and their little daughter, Rose Mary Moore Redfern, to the actual site of the Moore family massacre. After a three-hour drive south-west of Lexington, we arrived at Abb's Valley in remote, rural Tazewell County. There, by the roadside stands a sombre stone monument recounting part of the story of how the Indians swooped down on the Moore farm on the morning of July 14, 1786, killing many of the family and taking the rest into captivity, slaughtering most of them on the way to, or arrival in, their village in what is now the state of Ohio.

Led by local historian Michele Crigger, Wendy and I climbed up a steep Abb's Valley hill and entered into a deep woodland in search of some vestige of the horrific events. Using her staff to push away earth and leaves, Michele revealed an embedded stone marker which stated that this was the place where Captain James Moore, a Revolutionary War veteran and Mary Moore's father, was shot and scalped by the Shawnees and later buried by neighbors.

One of Mary's brothers and sisters met the same fate beside the now tranquil little stream flowing nearby as did another brother in the adjacent field. And Martha Evans, visiting the Moores on the fateful day, gave herself up to captivity when she wrongly thought an Indian had spotted her hiding beneath an area rock outcrop. This, in fact, proved fortunate for Mary as it was Martha Evans' brother, Thomas, who, after a two-year search, eventually found the captive girls and brought them back to Virginia along with Mary Moore's previously captured older brother, James.

As we stood viewing our surroundings, something quite mystical happened: two jet black horses suddenly burst into the woodland. One moved to my side, nuzzled my hand and offered his head to be stroked almost as if we had met before. I remembered that Captain Moore was renowned as a breeder of thoroughbred horses and that James had, in fact, been captured by this same band of Indians as he successfully attempted to resist their efforts to steal his father's prize stallion.

Both this story and the subsequent plight of Mary Moore and other members of her family are recounted in *The Captives of Abb's Valley: A Legend of Frontier Life*, written years after her death by her son, the Rev James Moore Brown. It's still in print and mandatory reading for her numerous descendants as are visits to New Providence Presbyterian Church Cemetery, near Walkerlands, as it is there that Mary Moore and her husband, the Rev Samuel Brown, pastor of the church and father of her numerous children, are buried beneath a tall, stone monument.

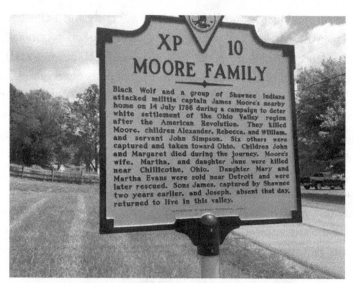

The Tazewell County roadside memorial to the Moore family

A New Life in New Jersey

My time in Virginia was also due to end, mercifully not as dramatically as that of the original Mary Moore, with the news that the Shephard brothers had split up, dividing their publishing business between them with *Holiday USA & Canada* sold to staffer and friend, Maureen Miller. As she had no journalistic background, Maureen urged me to return to London and help her relaunch the magazine; I thanked her but declined, believing the timing was not right. Instead, I temporarily left Mark with my mother and headed to New York in search of a place to live and employment.

Manhattan, I soon realized was too daunting for a single jobless mother and young child. Luckily, my old newspaper friend Rose Gilbert now lived in the attractive town of Maplewood, New Jersey, some 20 miles west of the Big Apple, so I bunked in with her and her two young sons, Scott and Bennett, until I could find a home to rent for Mark and me.

As Rose's specialty as a writer was home decorating, the house was delightfully eclectic, full of books, art work and collectibles, as well as a frisky cocker spaniel named Pugsly, two cats and various overnight house guests. Dark-haired, funny, an excellent writer and recently divorced from her intelligent but quite-mad husband, Rose had never met a stranger and parties cropped up on a whim.

Soon after my arrival I was summoned to an early breakfast to find the dining room decorated with crepe paper streamers and Rose, her two sons and even Pugsly adorned with party hats while the family housekeeper, her hair in rollers, earphones on, was belting out *Amazing Grace* while vacuuming the adjacent living room carpet.

"Hide, everyone hide," shouted Rose, "we want to surprise

Bernie – it's his birthday!" And as the boys and I ducked under the table, the mail man rang the bell, entered the door and found himself presented with a birthday cake topped with blazing candles. After his departure, I asked if was customary in Maplewood to hold surprise birthday parties for your mail man.

The answer was that she and Bernie had a special symbiotic relationship which originated from the sharing of their problems one cold, snowy morning. She had complained of the hefty early morning parking fees at the town train station from which she commuted into Manhattan; he complained about how he was carless and thus had to trudge through the snow on his postal route.

The solution was obvious: Bernie would deliver Rose's mail first, drive her to the station, continue his route and then stop by her place to enjoy a nap and a sandwich prepared by the housekeeper before dropping off the car for pick-up at the station when parking was free.

With the help of Rose and her friend, Claire Degnan, Mark and I were soon moved into a comfortable duplex overlooking the town playground and park and I focused on finding home help so I could start job hunting. Discovering that a young woman called Mandy from my area of Virginia was keen to move up north and go to business school, I hired her as an au pair and found a local

Cocktail hour with Rose Gilbert

business college she could attend while Mark himself was in school. Tall and blonde with a breathy Marilyn Monroe voice, Mandy soon proved an asset; not only did Mark like her but half the men in Maplewood seemed to succumb to her charms. This proved very useful when we needed house repairs done, wine quickly delivered or my automobile serviced. Unfortunately, her apparently-respectable boyfriend then burgled our house.

After Mandy completed her business school course and moved to California, I placed an advert for a replacement au pair in Britain's *The Lady* magazine which specializes in providing butlers, nannies and the like for Britain's posher families. It was answered by Cathy, a diminutive and apparently quite demure young lady from Glasgow whom I interviewed at Victoria Station when visiting London. She soon joined us and became a great favorite with Mark, possibly because they were close to the same size and she certainly had a sense of fun.

However, things became complicated when Cathy formed a crush on my lodger, Steve, a staffer from a nearby college who was engaged to someone else. This culminated in a number of problems, including a major row during which she proceeded to throw many of his possessions out of an upstairs window in the dead of night. So I had to ask the apparently-innocent Steve to find lodging elsewhere.

Cathy, apparently out of boredom, also regularly entertained visits from the Jehovah's Witnesses, although she professed to be an ardent Catholic. However, their devotion to her salvation became quite useful when they chauffeured me around after Cathy totaled the family car – and was forgiven as both the police and the local mechanic confirmed that it was a mechanical problem.

Meanwhile, my new friend Claire gave Mark a little black-and-white kitten that I named Fred, in tribute to my former boss, Fred Tupper. As he grew, he became more and more formidable, taking a particular dislike to any visiting male friends. In fact, he loved crawling along the back of the couch where they might be sitting, purring in a friendly manner and then nipping them on the back of the neck. As a joke, we found a postcard featuring a photo of a cat, not unlike Fred, seated behind barbed wire with this message: "Beware! These Premises Guarded By An Attack Cat!" It was posted just beside the front door and later proved quite useful.

One icy day, returning from job hunting in Manhattan, I found that the connecting train I needed to take from Hoboken, New Jersey, to Maplewood was severely delayed. Finding myself seated next to a rather attractive fellow commuter who said he was in advertising, I accepted his invitation to while away the time at a nearby bar. Then, when we arrived back at the station, he said: "I don't know why we are wasting our time here. My car is nearby. Let me drive you home – I go right past Maplewood."

Not stopping to ponder why this car owner was then spending time chatting me up in the train station, I enthusiastically accepted his offer but as we sped down the icy highways, he started to run his hand up and down my thigh and I began to wonder about the wisdom of my decision. When we arrived at my house I thanked him, hopped out of the car and started up the icy front steps. "But aren't you going to invite me in?" he asked, following me up the steps, pinning me against the front door and stroking the back of my neck.

"I really can't," I said, half jokingly pointing at the Attack Cat sign. "My cat wouldn't like it." He persevered, nudging me backwards as I opened the door and then I saw Fred across the room, his back arched, a hissing sound emerging from his jaws. Like John Wayne attacking his foes, he raced across the room and leapt on my admirer attaching his claws to his groin. Falling backwards with Fred on board he slid down the steps toward his car as

Fred, the attack cat

I sweetly said: "I told you so!" (Later, Fred moved in with my mother at Walkerlands where he was upstaged by her elegant Persian cat, Missy, who proved to be a better mouser than he. Initially sullen, he eventually succumbed to her charms and they became the best of friends.)

A Halloween street party in downtown Maplewood, New Jersey

Rose Gilbert (at front) with Maplewood house guests Claire Degnan and Michael Leech

Job Hunting in Manhattan

Although job hunting initially proved challenging, my old friend Morag came to the rescue. Having established her own Manhattan PR agency, she required temporary help promoting the *Operation Raleigh* youth charities of Colonel John Blashford-Snell. Then, Lou Hammond, a former Pan Am colleague, hired me to promote several of her clients, including a Spanish resort and Brooklyn Works, an organization promoting the businesses of that borough. So I found myself not only escorting journalists to Spain but also commuting to early-morning meetings in Brooklyn, in the process achieving some good media coverage for Manhattan's lively sister borough before my time with Lou was up.

A London friend stepped into the gap by persuading me to help her sell patriotic lollipops produced in France to a major New York City retailer. The time was ideal, she said, for a Statue of Liberty lollipop as 1986 was to be the year of the statue's centenary. Armed with a large effigy of the statue stuck on a stick I approached the relevant buyer in Macy's. "So what do you call that thing?" she snarled, as I entered her office and held it aloft. "Liberty Licks," I improvised, explaining that the lollipop, like the statue, was manufactured in France.

"I like it … but we would need it smaller. What's the price point? How many could you get in a container? And has it passed the Federal Drug Administration standards?" she queried. Unable to get any answers back from the French *artiste* who had created this and other patriotic lollipops (apparently the Eiffel Tower effigy had been a best seller in France), I decided to give it a miss.

Instead, I headed for an employment agency which, assuming I was seeking a secretarial position, insisted I take a typing test. After passing it and explaining my background, the interviewer said: "With your background, you shouldn't be looking for an office job;

you should become a consultant. The person who would love to meet you would be (and she named someone at the 92nd Street Y) as she is always looking for new program ideas."

Surprised to hear that there were so many B&Bs in Manhattan – Urban Ventures, which was run by one of my friends, on its own had more than 600 on its books – my new contact commissioned me to set up seminars for wealthy, bored empty-nesters, explaining how they could fill up their spare bedrooms and meet fascinating people from around the world. Soon, I was trekking around Manhattan, followed by note-taking ladies while we visited some of the homes of my B&B contacts – a splendid brownstone owned by a British expat; the chic apartment of a Broadway theatrical designer; and a rather camp Greenwich Village apartment occupied by two guys and their ribbon-festooned poodles.

Then I picked up the local newspaper and learned that a magazine called *Country Inns and Bed & Breakfasts* was to be launched in the neighboring town of South Orange. Soon I was regularly producing features for them about inns throughout the south and north-east as well as the UK and Ireland. Usually the research was uneventful but that proved not to be the case in Baltimore and western Ireland.

The idea for the Baltimore feature was to visit a downtown inn that regularly staged Agatha Christie-style murder mystery weekends. The inn's PR was expected to set up an impressively-staged event for me to write about and an accompanying photographer to film. However, when we arrived, we discovered that the pregnant PR – in premature labor – had been rushed off to the hospital and nothing had been done. Presented with a script but no cast, we had to improvise.

Luckily my friend Gonzalee happened to be in town and was transformed into a gipsy fortune teller and, with the aid of another old friend, Danute, now married and resident in Baltimore, we rounded up a group of shoppers from the local 7-Eleven with the promise of being in a photo shoot in the inn's rather grand parlor.

Finding a suitably atmospheric guest room, we set it up for a sinister scene complete with guttering candles and an ominous mask, tarot cards and a blood-red rose laid out on the four-poster bed. Then, taking a short break, we returned to find a distraught receptionist – forgetting we were photographing the room, she had ushered several would-be guests there. Seeing the scene, they fled from the premises in horror.

As for the Irish assignment, I was assured by the magazine publisher that although Irving, the selected photographer, primarily shot only in Manhattan studios, he was a nice reliable Jewish guy who would certainly be up to the job. But when I arrived at the modest Dublin B&B where we were due to overnight, the landlady, quite miffed, said Irving had arrived and refused to check in. Apparently her place was not up to his standards.

Asked about his whereabouts she explained he probably had gone to the local pub but as it was always crammed I might have trouble finding him. "Trust me," I replied, "I will have no problem spotting an unhappy New Yorker in the midst of an Irish pub." And there Irving was, dressed in a black roll-neck sweater and black trousers and gingerly perched on a bar stool. He couldn't believe, he moaned, that we were expected to overnight in such primitive accommodation – it didn't even have a proper power shower – and that he, a non-drinker, was forced to harbor in a pub and with such a terrible backache.

Commiserating, and once against improvising, I explained that one of the beauties of Irish pubs was that they also sold medicine. Ordering him a large Guinness, I announced that although it might be unpalatable it was therapeutic and he should perhaps have a second one before facing an overnight without a power shower.

The next day we headed to a Galway inn famed for its cooking school, where Irving irritated the chef by spraying shaving cream on the top of her freshly-baked pie – it withstood the heat of his lights better than cream, he explained. And at another inn, the staff watched through the window with amazement as every morning, being a fitness fanatic, Irving raced around the gardens. "What's he running from?" they asked. "Who knows?" I replied.

Back in Maplewood, I regularly visited Gonzalee, who had set up and was running a treasure-filled Manhattan antique shop known as Model T, and another former Richmonder, Sue Williams Krost, a one-time Miss Virginia in the Miss America competition, who was running a fashion and home-furnishing promotional business. On many a weekend Mark and I accompanied Sue and her son, Luke, into the enchanting Catskill Mountains, where we camped out in the rustic cabin she had converted into a weekend home and frequented the colorful local auction houses, where I bought most of the furniture for my new home in Maplewood.

Rose, Gonzalee and Sue also accompanied me to Walkerlands, where I helped my mother deal with the pasture rentals, negotiated with the loggers who annually did selective timbering in our hardwood forest, and then decided to do something about the derelict wooden building sitting on a hilltop at the edge of our land. Suspecting it might encase a log cabin, I offered to help fund new uniforms for the county high school baseball team if they would strip off the boards.

And there it was: a picturesque old cabin made of hand-hewn logs. Discovering that the tin roof was still sound and that a local man was an expert in log-cabin restoration, I hired him to rechink the logs, repair the stone foundation, install a bathroom and kitchen, rewire the cabin, build a vaulted upstairs ceiling and a front porch, run water in from a nearby spring and embed an underground septic tank. Then Mark, mother and I sat on the cabin's front porch admiring the view over Walkers' Creek before I handed over the keys to our first tenant, a local bluegrass musician.

Mother frequently accompanied me back to London and on one occasion calmly announced mid-way to Washington-Dulles International Airport that she had left her transatlantic ticket at the farm. I thought I dealt with the news rather calmly, suggesting several logical options but mother's response was: "You wouldn't be so snippy with me, missy, if you knew the secret I have been holding back from you ever since your daddy died." Alarmed, I pulled over to the side of the road and considered the possibilities. Was I an illegitimate child? Did I have an awful inherited disease? Had mother committed some terrible crime?

"I have been lying about my age," she finally admitted, explaining that her advanced age might explain why she forgot her ticket. And when I laughed, she added: "It's no laughing matter. The Feds are on to me and I might be arrested when I go through passport control."

It seems that when she last renewed her passport at the American Embassy in London the clerk asked why she had whited out her birth date – this was a federal offence which could result in a fine or prison sentence. Alarmed, my mother explained defensively to the clerk that she was older than my father and didn't want anyone to know. Noting mother's advanced age, the clerk said, "Well, by now couldn't you tell your husband?" "No," was my mother's response, "he's dead." Well, said the clerk, the problem is solved and after mother promised never to deface her passport again, it was renewed.

However, I still had to reassure her that being apprehended at the border was unlikely, and when – at her 95th birthday party at Walkerlands several years later – she was presented with a cake decorated with her age she announced to the guests that my memory was not as good as it should be. She was actually only 93.

One thing I definitely had not forgotten was how much I missed London, my stepchildren and my British friends, in spite of all my adventures and misadventures back in my native land. Also, I thought it was time for Mark, now 13, to spend more time with his father, Simon and Bridget. So when the opportunity arose, I grasped it with both hands.

A London Return and Texas Adventures

The opportunity to return came at London's *World Travel Market* in November of 1989 when I was asked by old friend Ian Raitt of the Raitt-Orr PR agency to join him in a meeting with the Texas tourism director. The meeting, in Ian's office near Victoria Station, went well as we shared the director's desire to promote his remarkable "Lone Star State", Ian's desire to help him do it, and my stories of press trips I had organized and accompanied to Texas in my Braniff days. But then the director told Ian that as much as he liked him and his company, he could not hire them as nobody on the staff had ever been to Texas. Calling for a coffee break, Ian whisked me into the office kitchen, offered me a job as the Texas account executive with a tempting salary; I accepted, and we got the account.

The following winter, Mark and I moved back to London, where he spent more time with his father, Bridget, now 23, and Simon, 24. We settled in happily to the attractive maisonette I purchased on the edge of once-gritty, now chic and trendy, Notting Hill, and he became a student at the American School in London, where he made friends from around the world.

My Texas "passport"

As in my Braniff days, media trips to Texas proved to be memorable, partly because the Texans, with their rather broad sense of humor, loved taking the piss out of the Brits and the Brits, in return, found the Texans not only larger than life but excellent copy.

Invited to attend a "cowboy morning breakfast" on the edge of the northern Panhandle's scenic Palo Duro Canyon, we arrived by chuck wagon to discover that the event was to begin with a cow patty-tossing competition. And when we dropped by for a trail ride at a Dallas area dude ranch, we were met by its middle-aged, voluptuous manager, crammed into tight jeans and crowned by a pink Stetson adorned with ostrich feathers – she could have been a Hollywood stand-in for Dolly Parton's granny. Gesturing to two flanking, overweight cowboys, she said: "Well hello, folks. I'm Big Lil and these are the boys."

I then explained that whereas most of us were relative horse-riding novices, we had among us a skilled equestrian, John Ruler, the travel writer for *Horse & Hounds,* who should be given a particularly fine horse. Unknown to me, the cowboys then put burrs under the saddle, so when John mounted and plopped down on the saddle his horse reared up with a snort and threw him into the sagebrush. Thankfully, John claimed to find it funny.

Strolling along San Antonio's picturesque River Walk, the decision was made to pop into a bar where we found a pianist, his eyes shadowed by a slouch hat, a cigarette tangling from his lips as he tinkled the keys. "I say, old chap," said one of the journalists in a cut-glass British accent, "Could you play *Danny Boy* for me?" "Fucking Limeys ... they're fucking Limeys," shouted the pianist, leaping up from the piano stool and hollering: "Let's get 'em, boys!" And we fled speedily from what was obviously an Irish-American pub.

Although the British media loved to write stories about the state's cowboys, dude ranches and feisty "Remember the Alamo" culture, I was also asked by the Texas tourism authorities to direct travel writers and broadcasters toward its numerous other attractions. Among them were big, vibrant modern cities such as Dallas and Houston, impressive art museums, the unique Tex-Mex cuisine, beautiful old Spanish missions in and around San Antonio, and its music heritage, particularly that centered on Austin. And that was not to forget the state's little-known, far south-west Big Bend and far north-central Panhandle regions or the attractive Gulf of Mexico coastline anchored by historic Galveston. Once a pirates' lair – and in the 1880s known as "The Wall Street of the South" – Galveston is still full of handsome Victorian buildings in spite of the devastation of the hurricane in 1900 that is still considered America's worst-ever natural disaster.

I was also asked to organize special themed events in London. Hence, "Big Blooming Texas", launched in the Chelsea Physic Garden and featuring a video by President Johnson's widow, Lady Bird, a great advocate of wild flowers not only in her native Texas but along the highways and parkways throughout America, and "Texas Is for the Birds", aimed at Britain's myriad of bird watchers.

What's Special about Texas?

Discounting Alaska, which is tacked on to the side of Canada in the far north-west, Texas is the largest of American contiguous states ... so large that several European countries could snuggle down within its borders. It's also the only American state that was once an independent country – between March, 1836, when it gained its independence from Mexico, and February, 1845, when it became America's 28th state (to then secede as part of the Confederacy from 1861–1870). This swashbuckling spirit of independence was exemplified by the exploits of the often-ruthless Ewing family in the popular 1978–1991 TV series *Dallas* and the 1956 film *Giant*, starring Rock Hudson, James Dean and Elizabeth Taylor. It's still reflected in Texas's local and national politics.

The Aga Khan and Italian Idylls

Meanwhile, another former Pan Am colleague, who was now heading up the London office of the Aga Khan's Italian-based airline Meridiana, asked me to help him promote its London-Florence and other expanding routes into Italy and elsewhere. Based upon this relationship, I was then approached with a job offer by another PR agency, Michael Joyce. It already represented the Aga Khan's various business interests and now needed a tourism expert to promote his five-star hotels sited throughout Europe.

As I had spent so many years promoting American destinations and airlines, I thought the change would be interesting so left Raitt-Orr and Texas for Michael Joyce and the Aga Khan's CIGA hotel group, retaining my involvement with Meridiana. My boss was Nick Hewer, whose other clients included technology tycoon Alan (now Lord) Sugar, who later starred in the British version of TV's *The Apprentice*, already fronted in the USA by New York businessman and future US President Donald Trump. By Sugar's side in the programs was Nick, who went on to be a popular TV presenter in his own right.

First, I set out to discover more about the Aga Khan. Also known as Prince Shah Karim al-Husayni and a descendant of the prophet Muhammad, he was not only the leader of the large Nizan Ismaili community of Shia Muslims, but also an immensely wealthy businessman, a philanthropist and a successful racehorse owner. His father was the Aly Khan, the third of Hollywood actress Rita Hayworth's five husbands.

Aided by two multi-lingual assistants, my job was to promote and organize press trips to the CIGA Hotels the Aga Khan owned in such alluring cities as Florence, Venice, Milan, Rome and

Vienna, as well as to Paris' prestigious Prix de Arc de Triomphe horse races featuring a number of the Aga Khan's horses. Meanwhile, I would continue to promote Meridiana's existing routes to Florence and Sardinia as well as new and often short-lived routes to places such as Verona, Turin and Barcelona. The most challenging project proved to be arranging for and accompanying journalists from five different countries to a grand relaunch of CIGA's two Vienna and three Milan hotels. Included in the program were tours of both cities, opulent banquets, a lovely evening of chamber music in Vienna and a night at Milan's renowned La Scala opera house.

After several years, I discovered that the Aga Khan planned to sell his hotel empire to the massive, international Sheraton group (it later became part of Marriott Hotels' Luxury Collection), which had its own in-house PR team, so I decided to take Mark with me on a farewell trip to some of my favorite hotels. Among them were Venice's palatial canal-side Danieli (we also dined in CIGA's equally majestic Gritti Place), Rome's Imperial, Paris's Meurice and Amsterdam's Pulitzer, set in a series of atmospheric, joined-together town houses.

Aware of Mark's teenage aversion to being marched through museums and historic palaces, I suggested a compromise: as soon as we reached the Hotel Danieli, we would obtain a copy of the local tourism magazine and each choose just one place to visit. His eyes lit up when he discovered there was a *Snoopy* exhibition in one of the city's historic buildings. So we jumped on a *vaporetto*, headed up the Grand Canal and found ourselves wandering past numerous cartoons of the misadventures of hapless Charlie Brown, bossy Lucy, Linus and the rest, plus a dog house for Snoopy, a cheeky little Woodstock perched on its roof. My contribution was the Peggy Guggenheim Museum, where both Mark and I enjoyed its outstanding array of modern art.

Amsterdam was another story. Sensing that Mark really didn't want to visit any museum, I used reverse psychology and told him we had no time to visit them. However, when we strolled past the

Rijksmuseum, he spotted a notice for an exhibition of World War I photography that he said he would quite like to see. I agreed, apparently reluctantly, and several hours later we emerged after cruising by Rembrandt's *Nightwatch* and numerous other masterpieces, later to visit the wonderful Van Gogh Museum.

Then after a visit to the incredibly moving Anne Frank House museum, I persuaded Mark to accompany me to the Little Church in the Attic, tucked away in the eaves of a townhouse, as was the Frank family's hiding place. I was surprised that he seemed to want to spend so much time in the place until I discovered that by looking out the window he could view several nude ladies sunbathing on the roof of a nearby building.

The Water Entrance to Venice's majestic Danieli Hotel, now part of Marriott Hotels' Luxury Collection

The Birth of Essentially America

In 1993, I was approached by my *Holiday USA & Canada* former colleague and friend Maureen Miller. Wasn't it about time, she asked, for us to relaunch the magazine, which she had kept alive but only as an annual USA tourism directory? So we drafted a plan. She would find financial, advertising and production support if I served – freelance at my request – as editorial director, writing and commissioning articles, accompanying her to travel trade shows and working with a designer to produce a quarterly publication.

Armed with flip charts indicating that the time was ripe to produce such a publication as tourism to North America was rapidly growing, we organized a meeting with the relevant executive of the powerful, nationwide WH Smith news-stand organization. There, we met with a young woman executive who, apparently bored by our presentation, said: "I really don't understand what this publication is all about." Losing my cool, I smacked my hand on the table and rather sarcastically said: "Well, *essentially* it's about America!" "Essentially America, I like the name," she mused.

"How brilliant of you to come up with that name; that's what we'll call it," said Maureen, kicking me under the table. And in February, 1994, the first issue of *Essentially America* rolled off the press, featuring on the cover an exuberant female skier and such strap lines as *California Wine with Oz Clark* and *Sleeping with the Americans*, a tribute to the wealth of unusual, sometimes quirky, bed & breakfasts available throughout the USA.

Ensconced with a small staff in a former warehouse in the once down-market Old Street area of London, we beavered away establishing the profile and position of *Essentially America*, aided by a series of freelance designers, most of them outside London. I found myself traveling to such places as a Kent oast house, used in the beer-brewing process, where I worked alongside our two designers, a large dog and an illustrator of horror-fiction books, and, later, with a larger team at Cambridge Publishing based in its namesake university city.

From the third issue onwards in 1994, Maureen was ably assisted at *Essentially America* by Connecticut-based advertising guru Larry Cohen, and the magazine expanded into producing sponsored guides to various cities, states and regions while I wrote or commissioned stories on everything from *North America's Secret Beaches* and *Mark Twain's Hannibal, Missouri* to a Manhattan detective story feature called *Sleuthing Through the Skyscrapers* and another on *Islands with a Southern Accent*.

Along the way, Maureen, a horse racing fan, bought a racehorse, which was adorned with *Essentially America* trappings – unfortunately, it did not live up to expectations – and then we both were invited to Louisville's Kentucky Derby. Carried away by the occasion, Maureen purchased an extraordinarily expensive and flamboyant hat that, alas, she set on fire while chain-smoking in the Churchill Downs VIP area. The waiter saved the day – but not the hat – by spraying it vigorously with a soda siphon. And I managed to redeem our reputation by placing a few winning bets based upon tips I had picked up while attending Aga Khan-sponsored racing events.

Often traveling to North American destinations with other more-fit and fearless British travel writers, I discovered that we were sometimes expected to indulge in perilous pursuits for which I was ill-suited. I had already been told by one travel writer friend how he suffered broken bones after losing control of a dog sled in Colorado and by another about experiencing whiplash from an abortive bungee jump somewhere in the USA.

So my internal alarm system immediately went off in the Canadian Rockies when a jolly PR lady crowned me with a crash helmet, dressed me in gear so

With Maureen Miller at a stud farm en route to the Kentucky Derby

padded that I looked like a Michelin Man and summoned me toward the off-road vehicle I was expected to race down a rutted, rocky cliff-side mountain track. Discovering, not for the first time, that creative cowardice was my best chance of survival, I announced that I would have to travel pillion with another driver as I always took notes in the middle of such a unique experience and obviously couldn't simultaneously scribble and steer.

The pillion option rose again – and succeeded – when, on Florida's Marco Island, I was instructed by another jolly PR lady to leap on a jet ski for the first time ever and zip down the Gulf of Mexico to the Ten Thousand Islands. There, she said, we would "have fun feeding marshmallows to the alligators". And then there was the occasion when I opted out of a sky-diving experience up the Florida coast by announcing that I was instead obligated to write about the nearby Naples Teddy Bear Museum (which, alas, no longer exists).

Why continue to be such a party pooper, I finally asked myself in a charming resort outside Ojai, California. So I joined the other journos in a quite amusing geo-caching expedition up a mountainside in intense early-summer heat and then hopped on a push bike for the first time since my teenage years to cycle into town.

The trip back up the steep hillside was quite exhausting and so it was a relief when, straggling behind the others, I turned the corner at the brow of the hill and raced down the other side to return the bike. Then, to my horror, I saw my buddies standing in the middle of the bike path and had to make a decision: swerve to the left and run into the side of a cliff, swerve to the right and go over another cliff, or put on the brakes. Suddenly, I was flying through the air and was relieved to find myself apparently in one piece when I hit the ground. "I'm just fine," I called out to my colleagues. "Well then, you'll be needing these," said my travel writing friend Sarah Tucker, handing me my two-and-a-half front teeth.

Badly bruised on my face, right arm and leg, I spent the next afternoon in the operating room of a local dentist who had a puckish sense of humor. "Ladies," he said to his assistants, "this is Miss Mason, a famous kick boxer from Britain who took on our local champion and obviously met her match." With my mouth full of metal equipment, there was no way to refute his story so I had to endure the pitying glances of his team while he chortled to himself. My new teeth were splendid but I decided this was the end of any further derring-do.

(Shortly before the Covid-19 pandemic lockdown one tooth fell out in a London restaurant. As no dentists were available at the time I flew to America looking the worse for wear, waiting until my return to London months later to have it replaced. Luckily few on the flights or on the ground noticed the difference – thank goodness for those mandatory masks!)

Traumas, Tragedies and Triumphs

Then *Essentially America* faced its own traumatic experience. On September 11, 2001, having signed off that issue of the magazine, I was holidaying at Walkerlands when I heard the terrible news of the destruction and horrific death toll at Manhattan's Twin Towers. What were we to do? New York City was on the cover, with a light-hearted feature inside focusing on the appeal of Lower Manhattan, particularly the area around the Twin Towers. There was no time to write, commission, illustrate and lay out another feature.

After consulting with Maureen over the phone, it was decided to kill the Manhattan feature, expand a Canadian feature and replace the cover picture with a nice photo of Quebec City. There was just one problem: the photo was not ideal for our usual cover design, which ran all the subject lines down the left side, so we would have to flip the photo right to left. I tracked down the UK-based PR for Quebec and the response was immediate: "Of course, flip the photo. Nobody will notice, and it's great for Quebec City to be in such a prominent position."

Soon the American tourism destinations began to pull out their advertising on the assumption that the Brits would now be too fearful of future attacks to visit America. Gradually, they were persuaded that with their famous World War II "stick it to the enemy" spirit, the British would keep soldiering on. However, Maureen was not convinced she could.

Facing some health and financial problems as well as the desire of her partner to move to New Zealand where his daughter now lived, Maureen began to search discreetly for a way out. And in January, 2002, she sold Phoenix International Publishing and *Essentially America* to UK-based Mick Shires and his Texas-based friend, Simon Todd, both former travel industry colleagues. The office was closed; all the staff were made redundant; I was the only survivor. And, within a matter of days, I was getting the next issue of *Essentially America* off to press from my spare bedroom in Notting Hill, now transformed into an office.

As Mick was the silent partner, I was now working long-distance with Simon, Connecticut-based Larry and, later, with a new design team based in Florida. We continued to not only run destinational features on American cities (*48 Hours in Denver*) and states (*Abe Lincoln's Illinois*) but also features about other parts of North America (*Canada's Most Alluring Small Towns; Discovering Frida Kahlo's Mexico City*). Then there were the profiles of individual Americans, ranging from Muhammad Ali to *Benjamin Franklin: America's Renaissance Man* and such thematic articles as *Swapping Homes with the Americans*; *North America's Most Seductive Spas* and *Theatre Under the Stars*.

Displaying the 50th issue of Essentially America *with more than 50 yet to come. (Photo: Geoff Moore)*

In 2006, I won a Visit USA award for Outstanding Media Contribution; in 2009, a similar award from the state of California; and, in 2010, the top travel writing award in a multi-national competition presented by the US Travel Association at its annual IPW conference in San Francisco. It was for *From Oz to Oklahoma*, a feature describing how popular culture added to the allure of the USA, in this case as exemplified by a new museum in small-town Wamego, Kansas, inspired by Frank Baum's *Wizard of Oz* and other *Oz* books, and by a Tulsa, Oklahoma, performance of Rodgers and Hammerstein's *Oklahoma*, one of the most enduring American musicals.

Then, in 2011, PIP began publishing a Spanish-language edition, distributed in Mexico and, later, in other Latin American countries, followed in 2012 by a Chinese edition and, in 2013, by a German edition, all including stories translated from the ones produced by our team of UK and USA freelance writers.

On the personal side of my life, Mark, who had long been fascinated by films, TV and music, had graduated with a film degree from the University of Southern California in Los Angeles, worked for a while in the Hollywood film industry and later married his photographer sweetheart, Wendy Lynch, on the top of Big Bear Mountain near LA. The two of them launched – and still edit and publish – *Under the Radar*, an indie music magazine.

My stepdaughter, Bridget, married (and later divorced) musician/actor Chris Brooker who, at the time, was starring in the popular West End musical *Return to the Forbidden Plane*, and they had two daughters, Eleanor and Isobel; and stepson Simon moved to New Zealand with his American girlfriend, Erin.

On January 2, 2013, I was visiting Mark and Wendy, then living at Walkerlands, in anticipation of the birth of their first child at the end of the month. Suddenly things took a dramatic and alarming turn: on Wendy's routine visit to her obstetrician that day we were

Mark and Wendy Redfern on their wedding day

told that the baby would have to be induced within hours and after Rose was born late that night we learned that she had one collapsed lung and a hole in the other. She was rushed by ambulance over the mountains to the University of Virginia's Neo-Natal Intensive Care unit in Charlottesville with Mark following behind in the family car.

I hitched a ride to a local hotel with an Afghan War veteran who was visiting the hospital and pondered over how I was going to get a frantic Wendy to Charlottesville within the next 24 hours though the doctor urged her to stay behind and rest. Luckily a family friend happened to be headed from Lexington to Charlottesville and ferried us there. As we spent an anxious week in the emergency ward I spent time in the waiting room on my computer trying to get that issue of *Essentially America* off to press. Luckily all went well and a healthy Rose returned with us all to Walkerlands.

Wendy with baby Rose

Rose, age 3, trying on dad's shoes

Meanwhile Simon, now an Internet technology expert who composed music in his spare time, had moved to Berlin where he was living with his delightful German partner, Evie, and their two children, Lara and Dominik. And Simon and Bridget's mother, Kate, with whom I had become great friends over the years, was now not only a skilled teacher but a talented and prolific artist. However, in October, 2014, David died after a long struggle with pancreatic cancer and in June of 2016, dear Bridget also died of cancer, leaving behind her now-teenage daughters, Isobel and Eleanor, and a devastated second husband, Mike Wattles.

Simon, Mark and Bridget Redfern
(Photo: David Redfern)

All the World's a Stage

Along the way, I became great friends with Michael Leech, a delightfully-dotty gay guy who wrote about the theater and restaurants as well as travel. He regularly invited me and his friend, Penny Jones, a radio journalist, not only for meals at his bijou flat tucked away in the eaves of a Covent Garden building but also for weekends to his Tudor-style cottage in the historic village of Sandwich.

One year, he also invited me to accompany him on a *Queen Elizabeth II* voyage to Manhattan with the British Guild of Travel Writers. When I arrived by taxi to collect Michael from his flat, I found him greatly agitated – he couldn't find the essential black shoes he needed to accompany his tuxedo and he complained that I had not arrived with a bottle of gin which we needed to entertain fellow Guild members in our stateroom.

A moment of merriment with Michael Leech

Even though he was assured that we could buy both shoes and gin in Southampton before we boarded the ship, Michael remained flustered. When we arrived at the port city, he rushed into a local shoe shop, shouting at the assistant: "Quick, quick, I need a bottle of gin!" Once on board, he discovered his tuxedo was uncomfortably snug but, nevertheless, we arrived in considerable style in the grand ballroom where Michael was seated next to the elegantly-adorned, much-younger second wife of one of our members.

Recounting a hilarious story with a sweep of his hand, he overturned a carafe of red wine into her lap. Greatly embarrassed, he began mopping it from her crotch; she rose up in high dudgeon and swept out of the room, with Michael, apologizing profusely, trotting after her. Halfway across the ballroom his pants split and cascaded toward the floor. Later, he returned with a brand new pair of tuxedo trousers – only on the *QEII* could you make such a purchase at 9 o'clock at night. Madam of the wine-soaked crotch was thereafter noticeable by her absence.

Later on the voyage, I ventured into another ballroom and was asked to dance by one of the "gentlemen hosts". As we glided around the ballroom floor, he explained in a TV-worthy New Jersey accent that he and his fellow hosts were given free passage on ships in return for dancing and chatting with the unaccompanied lady passengers. However, he assured me, visits to their staterooms was totally forbidden. "What was your previous profession," I asked. "I was a Catholic priest," he responded, "but it transpired that my services were no longer needed." I wondered why.

Among the lecturers on board was renowned travel writer Bill Bryson, whose first travel book, *The Lost Continent: Travels in Small-Town America*, was a favorite of mine. When I asked him and his wife to join Michael, me and a few other travel writers for afternoon tea, he revealed that his next book would be about hiking down America's more-than 2,000-mile-long Appalachian Trail. With great audacity, I announced that I thought it was a bad idea. "You are such a people person, Bill," I said, "and you probably won't meet many people by walking through the woods … just squirrels, snakes and perhaps the occasional bear." Listening politely, he mentioned that he might take a friend along. His book inspired Hollywood's 2015's *A Walk in the Woods*, which starred Robert Redford as Bryson and Nick Nolte as his unfit, overweight but droll friend Stephen Katz.

Becoming increasingly impressed by the work of the Guild and the talent of many of its members, I later joined, became a member of its executive committee and, in 2010, as vice chairman, worked with its chairman, Roger Bray, to produce *We Were There*, a booklet celebrating the role Guild members had played in key tourism events during its first 50 years.

In 2014 I became the Guild's first American chairman at a time when it faced many challenges: it needed to be transformed into a Limited Liability Company; the website's design was past its prime; adjustments were required for the increasing number of online travel writers; and a lawsuit from a disgruntled member had to be successfully concluded. But there were also the benefits of the great professional contacts and camaraderie, the splendid AGMs held in places as diverse as Oman, Tenerife and East Germany, and the gala annual awards dinner at the splendid Savoy hotel, two of which I presided over.

Presiding over a British Guild of Travel Writers' Yearbook launch

One of these, sponsored by my contacts in the Louisiana Office of Tourism, was memorable for both its excellent New Orleans-inspired cuisine and its live music. The other, for a totally different reason: as it was sponsored by the Armenia tourism authority, I was required to make an introductory speech about a country I had never visited.

Deciding to focus instead on famous people of Armenian extraction, I prepared what I considered a witty speech about entertainers Charles Aznavour, Cher and the Kardashians, as well as wealthy, eccentric bon vivant Nubar Gulbenkian (who had once resided at the Savoy), only to discover when I arrived at the Savoy the evening of the event that the hosts, without previously informing us, would be providing their own film about famous home-grown Armenians (most of whom we had never heard of). Therefore, my prepared speech was to be replaced by another one hastily written by somebody else.

Alas, there was no opportunity for me to rehearse this from the stage as it was occupied by an Armenian band that had suddenly materialized and was fronted by a man whose skill was making musical sounds by blowing into a bottle. Then, as I ascended the stage, I discovered that the tele-prompters had been set about a foot too low for me and, as I crouched to read from them, the zipper at the back of my ball gown broke. Nobody seemed to notice as by then they were all well reinforced by the strong Armenian brandy being served at each table.

Not all of my attention was focused on publishing and the travel business. Over the years I had served as co-chair and chairman of West London's Hereford Road street association, which provided many opportunities to mingle with fellow residents, community leaders and politicians while dealing with sometimes-challenging local situations.

And, in 1993, I became involved in bringing our local landmark Anglican church back to life. Built in 1856, neo-Gothic St Stephen's Westbourne Park had remained boarded up and depressingly derelict for several years due to its structural problems and diminished congregation. Then Holy Trinity, a larger, wealthier Anglican church, sent in a restoration team and called for local volunteers.

When we arrived at the church, my friend and I discovered it full of everything from broken chairs to ancient church artifacts; birds fluttered around the eaves, their droppings encrusting the pews; plaster was peeling off the damp walls and there were cracks in the floor. As for the once impressive steeple, it had been shot off by friendly fire in World War II, leaving behind a still-impressive tower.

Miraculously, a sizeable grant was obtained from the National Heritage Fund, work proceeded and, although still a building site, St Stephen's began holding services again over Easter, 1995. Then, on February 11, 2002, when the church was mercifully empty, a mentally disturbed man drove his Volvo through the front door and sped into the sanctuary, causing havoc along the way. Summoned by neighbors, the police then found him parked beside the altar calmly reading *The Sunday Times*. So more repairs needed to be made.

As it evolved, the church not only became a hub of community activities but also attracted parishioners who were originally from places as varied as Australia, New Zealand, the Caribbean, Africa, Sir Lanka, and Scandinavia. This diversity really came into play when we began to organize our first major nativity play. One of our number, an energetic Irishman named Bill Hargreaves, summoned a number of us on to a committee, which I agreed to join, although – aware of my previous nativity play misadventures – in a limited capacity; I would assemble the props.

Tiffany Jackson (left) and Clare Allcock celebrating British heritage at St Stephen's

Bill's vision was that we should focus on both the divisive world of Jesus's time and that of our current times. A plinth would be constructed in the center of the church and on it would be the Father, portrayed by Andy, a tall, stately church leader; the Son, by Roland, a handsome younger church member; and the as-yetuncast Holy Spirit. I raised my hand and suggested that for diversity the Holy Spirit should be portrayed by a woman. One of our members, a lapsed Catholic, protested: "The Holy Spirit is always portrayed by a dove!"

As I explained that a trained dove was hard to find, one of our Nigerian lady members announced in a loud voice: "I wants to be the Holy Spirit," and that was that. Another lady stated that her baby – a little girl – should be the infant Jesus and yet another member, who ran a local dance group, proposed that her students, with long scarves floating behind them, should waft through the church representing the Spirits of the Earth.

Other characters to be included – all powerful voices for morality – were to be Martin Luther King, Gandhi and Mother Teresa; due to a lack of an adequate number of male volunteers, God the Father and Jesus the Son would need to double as two of the three Wise Men. Silhouettes of teenagers fighting amongst themselves behind a back-lit screen would represent the violence of modern-day life and children in the church would portray the animals around the manger. Inexplicably noticeable by their absence were any angels and shepherds.

After assembling and delivering the various required props, I left London on a travel writing trip, only to return three days before the event to a phone ringing off the hook. Picking it up, I heard the rather agitated voice of the vicar, Tom Gillum. "Where are the costumes, Mary?" he asked. " The play is almost upon us and you were meant to provide the costumes." "No, Tom," I responded, "I provided the props. Surely there must be some costumes in the church from previous nativity plays." But when we opened the storage trunk, there were only various lengths of cloth plus a few costumes for child angels.

An emergency meeting was called. Cassocks were found for several cast members, including the Virgin Mary and Mother Teresa. Gandhi absolutely refused to wear the dhoti I contrived for him out of various scraps of material and ended up in a sarong, and Jo, the vicar's wife, and I decided to clothe the Three Kings in our ornate kaftans. They were then made regal by Cinderella crowns I purchased from the children's section of a local department store. As they processed down the central aisle one participant was heard to whisper snidely: "Here come the three queens."

And as the animals assembled around the crèche, they included not only a donkey and a sheep but also a kangaroo, tiger and zebra. Then, miraculously, angels appeared in the form of a group of rather bossy little girls who, hearing of the event, wanted to participate. As one had just come from a costume party, she wore an alien antenna rather than a tinsel halo. In the end, everyone watching the production indicated that this was the most memorable nativity play they had ever seen.

Now a member of the Parish Church Council, I helped St Stephen's celebrate its 150th anniversary in 2006 by writing and editing a special commemorative magazine. This process was repeated in 2018 after the church once again faced structural challenges and obtained support from the National Lottery Heritage Fund.

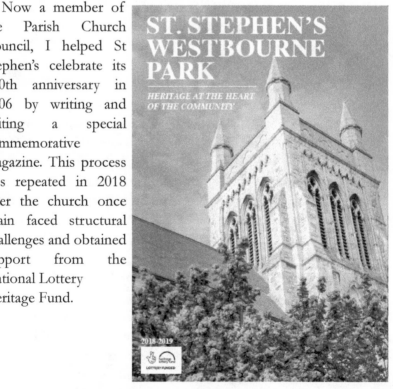

ST. STEPHEN'S WESTBOURNE PARK

HERITAGE AT THE HEART OF THE COMMUNITY

2018-2019

Awards and Those Unforgettable
Road Trips

In March, 2018, *Essentially America* was sold to Tobias Zerr, a Chicago-based online publisher who greatly enhanced its website and, in 2019, launched a new print edition into the four Nordic countries as well as financing a festive London party celebrating the 25th anniversary of the founding of the publication.

That same year I achieved my goal of visiting all 50 American states by adding Nebraska and North Dakota to my roster and was given media awards in London by the Visit USA association and, at its St Louis, Missouri, convention, by the Travel South organization representing 12 Southern states. When asked later what is was for, I answered: "Durability ... lasting the course."

In retrospect, it is always difficult to decide which city, state, region or, indeed, visit has made the most lasting impression on me. As a native Virginian who also lived in five other Southern states, the American South is probably the region I know best. It is a region of wonderful, colorful stories as well as of dark and tragic history.

Among my more bizarre experiences was attendance at the "birth" of my very own

Accepting the 2019 Visit USA media award
(Photo: Tracey Spuyman)

Cabbage Patch Kid at northern Georgia's hilltop Babyland General Hospital. After the "baby" was pulled from one of the "delivery room's" massive felt cabbages, I was ushered into a separate room to sign official adoption papers during which I was sternly reminded by the "lawyer" that this was not a doll but a kid. Later, I was introduced to two very butch middle-aged gents, one a police chief from California, who between them had adopted and were living with hundreds of such "kids" – apparently they are greatly sought after as valuable collectibles.

Then there were such flamboyant events as a re-enactment of a New Orleans Mardi Gras parade where, dressed as a jester, I rode on one of the floats; the Kentucky Derby lunch party where I sat next to the then Miss America, who just happened to be married to the state's Lieutenant Governor; and an *American Queen* cruise up the mighty Mississippi River, stopping at such lovely Deep South towns as Natchez and St Francisville as well as at a number of beautiful, white-columned plantation mansions.

But it was also important to tell the story of the enslaved people who lived in the cabins behind those mansions; of the now-tranquil Civil War battlefields which were once drenched with the blood of thousands of young Northern and Confederate soldiers; of such grim events as the 1963 Ku Klux Klan bombing of the 16th Street Baptist Church in Birmingham, Alabama, killing four young African American girls and wounding 22 other people; and of not only the Civil Rights movement but also of the 2018 Civil Rights Trail, which testifies to the sacrifice and bravery of those who fought to make America a better, fairer place – still reflected in today's Black Lives Matter protests.

Moving away from the Deep South to the Far North, in the winter of 2016 I joined hundreds of spectators for the ceremonial launch of Alaska's famous Iditarod dog-sled race.

Lining the icy streets of Anchorage, we cheered on 82 teams as they ceremonially began their race through some 1,000 miles of treacherous Alaskan terrain. Later, cups of steaming hot cider in hand, some of us sat outdoors watching in awe as the night sky became the technicolor spectacle of the Northern Lights.

I have always been fascinated by the rich and varied heritage of America's often-cruelly-treated native people. So it was a privilege to spend an evening in the mountains of North Carolina watching *Unto these Hills*, the outdoor dramatization of how some of the local Cherokees escaped the tragedy of President Andrew Jackson's late-1830s Indian Removal Act. And later, to visit the impressive Oklahoma settlements of those Cherokees who managed to survive the 1,200-mile march westward along what has become known as "The Trail of Tears".

Over the years, I have visited a number of New Mexico pueblos, including mesa-top Acoma, said to be the oldest continuously-inhabited place in America, and, on another trip, I met up in Salmon, Idaho, with the great, grand niece of Sacagawea, the famous Lemhi Shoshone woman who proved invaluable on the 1803-1806 Lewis and Clark expedition that opened up the western USA to exploration and settlement.

When I found myself marooned on a flooded back road near South Dakota's Wounded Knee, site of one of the most infamous massacres of aboriginal people, I was rescued by a truck-driving Native American school teacher, and, in 2019, when I visited Omaha, Nebraska, I was met at the airport by a Sioux Indian taxi driver among whose regular customers was the city's most-famous resident, billionaire Warren Buffet, and his wife, who, said my driver, particularly liked shopping at the local charity shop.

Although I am not a skilled equestrian, I found that horseback was a great way to explore the mountainsides of the Hawaiian island of Maui and Colorado as well as Antelope

Island in the midst of Utah's Great Salt Lake. And then there were the thrilling small-plane flights over the Manhattan skyscrapers and to the Chesapeake Bay island of Tangier, Virginia, still occupied by the descendants of its early 17th-century settlers.

So much is written about the vibrant downtown areas of such majestic cities as New York, Chicago and Los Angeles that it has been a treat to explore their outer reaches, such as the Big Apple's borough of Brooklyn, with its splendid Prospect Park, Brooklyn Museum and stunning views of the Manhattan skyline; Miami's elegant Coral Gables, home to the Venetian Pool and Fairchild Tropical Gardens; greater Los Angeles's Venice Beach and the tranquil inland canals that inspired its name; and Cambridge, just across the Charles River from Boston and home to world-renowned Harvard University.

Then there were the other parts of the states and regions reached through the great international gateway cities: the delightful small towns and coastal areas of the six New England states, all reached via Boston; the Great River Road along the Mississippi and legendary Route 66, both accessed from Chicago; the myriad of colorful communities all along Pacific Oceanside Route 1 stretching southwards from San Francisco; the palatial mansions, including that of President Franklin Delano Roosevelt, along the Hudson River north of Manhattan and, farther to the north, areas associated with the abolitionists, their slave-escape route known as the Underground Railway and the pioneering women who launched their lengthy battle for their right to vote, which celebrated its centenary in 2020.

Of course, not all my time was spent in the USA. There was also that magical evening when I sailed down the Nile as white egrets soared overhead and the call to prayer sounded from the minarets along the way; the starlit October night when I luxuriated in a natural hot pool in northern Iceland; the day I

A photo from the 2020 Essentially America *feature commemorating the centenary of American women getting the right to vote*

strolled with a friend along a 600-year-old portion of the Great Wall of China; and the afternoon I traveled in the back of a truck into a Jordanian desert where my Muslim guides pointed out that not only had Lawrence of Arabia passed through this area but that Moses had here been given a useful lecture on delegation by his father-in-law, Jethro, as recounted in *Exodus, Chapter 18.* And then there was that special occasion when I met the-then young – now late – Sultan Qaboos bin Said of Oman, learning his modernization plans for the future and then, as he became the Arab world's longest-serving ruler, returning to the country to find them impressively fulfilled.

Stuck in a truck in the Jordanian desert (Photo: Penny Jones)

Now, having won my Golden Girl credentials, I am back at Walkerlands awaiting the discovery of what's next in my life. Will I head off around the world to find new adventures in places I have never been before, fondly return to places I have learned to love over the years, or stay put for a while, turning Walkerlands into a family-run Airbnb while beginning work on another book and spending more time with granddaughter Rose Mary Moore Redfern?

Will there even continue to be travel writers and publications after travel was disrupted for so long during the pandemic... and what about the future of both the post-Brexit United Kingdom and the USA, so politically and emotionally torn apart during the four divisive Trump Years and now facing so many challenges as it struggles to return to a new and hopefully more progressive normal life under a new Democratic administration?

Rose Mary Moore Redfern, age 7,
as Wonder Woman